NEGRO LEADERSHIP IN A SOUTHERN CITY

NEGRO LEADERSHIP IN A SOUTHERN CITY

by

M. Elaine Burgess

Chapel Hill

THE UNIVERSITY OF NORTH CAROLINA PRESS

To my own special power structure—
"The House of Burgesses"

ACKNOWLEDGMENTS

THIS project has benefited from the advice and assistance of many individuals. During the initial stages of inquiry, Guy B. Johnson, Reuben Hill, and Gordon W. Blackwell provided able support. Rupert B. Vance, Daniel O. Price, Charles E. Bowerman, Richard L. Simpson, and Harriet J. Kupferer have read the manuscript in whole or in part. For their interest, encouragement, criticisms, or suggestions I am deeply grateful. Dr. Vance is due a more special acknowledgment for helping to set this study in proper perspective. Whatever shortcomings there may be in the final product are, of course, my own responsibility.

I wish to express my appreciation to the Institute for Research in Social Science of the University of North Carolina for financial assistance in preparation of the study and to the Woman's College for its continuing support. I owe a very special debt of gratitude to Robert Agger, whose interest in the project led him to provide funds for field work in the Negro community.

I am also indebted to the staff of The University of North Carolina Press, from whom I have received many valuable suggestions for improving the manuscript.

I wish to acknowledge my indebtedness to the Ford Foundation for generous aid in the publication of this book by a grant under its program for assisting American university presses in the publication of works in the humanities and the social sciences.

Finally, I wish to thank all of those individuals in "Crescent City" who took time from busy lives to cooperate with this research project. I am particularly grateful to members of the sub-community who assisted in many ways. Need for anonymity prevents my naming them. While not all of them will agree with what I have said, I hope they will receive the study as a sincere attempt to shed further light on the complex problems of race and power relations.

CONTENTS

CONTENTS

LIST OF TABLES

LIST OF FIGURES

NEGRO LEADERSHIP IN A SOUTHERN CITY

CHAPTER I

RACE RELATIONS AS POWER RELATIONS: AN INTRODUCTION

A LITTLE over a decade ago, in his presidential address before the American Sociological Association, E. Franklin Frazier urged his colleagues to develop broader and more meaningful research in race relations. Man has been intrigued with studies of race and ethnic phenomena over the past century. Yet in the twelve years since Frazier expressed a concern shared by many others, there has been more valuable analysis in the field than ever before. Concepts and approaches of a generation or two ago are now considered inadequate. Studies stressing value declarations, deterministic notions, or pure description have gradually given way to those drawing upon concepts, hypotheses, and findings from other areas of the social sciences. The speed with which majority-minority relations are changing throughout the world, coupled with our changing knowledge about these relations, makes us aware that our progress has been small indeed. But, hopefully, a growing research interest in theoretical developments will integrate race relations into a gradually developing theory of human behavior.

A current point of departure that is especially promising views majority-minority relations as an aspect of power relations. Explanations of prejudice and discrimination, of cooperation, accommodation, and conflict, can be found, among other places, in the power arrangements of our society, for it is often the strategy of organized interest groups, rather than the normative system or the psychological dimensions of prejudice, that seems to control behavior. I am in no sense implying that minority-majority affairs can be viewed entirely as maneuvers for power. Power is not the sole explanation, but it is one of several factors to be taken into account. And it isn't necessary to decide which set of factors is "dominant" in order to realize the importance of power groupings.[1]

In the study of race and power relations, the community is the research setting. It is only recently that social scientists have moved to the local level to observe these relationships.[2] Yet such phenomena can very fruitfully be observed on this level. Changing social relationships between the majority-minority groups can, for example, best be analyzed within the context of community organization and institutional structure. Current decisions within the biracial community on such major issues as desegregation can bring into bold relief the process of the exercise of power and the making of decisions.

An urban center known for the purposes of this book as "Crescent City" was chosen as the study site. Located in

1. Brief theoretical discussions of this approach are included in the following sources: Robin M. Williams, Jr., "Race and Cultural Relations," in *Review of Sociology*, ed. J. P. Gittler (New York: John P. Wiley and Sons, 1957), p. 451; George E. Simpson and J. Milton Yinger, *Racial and Cultural Minorities* (Rev. ed.; New York: Harper and Brothers, 1958), p. 70; R. A. Schermerhorn, *These Our People* (Boston: D. C. Heath and Co., 1949), pp. 7-10; Joseph S. Roucek, "Minority-Majority Relations in Their Power Aspects," *Phylon*, 17 (First Quarter, 1956), 25-30; J. P. Lohman and D. C. Reitzes, "Note on Race Relations in Mass Society," *American Journal of Sociology*, LVIII (November, 1952), 242.

2. See, for example, E. Franklin Frazier, "Race Contacts and the Social Structure," *American Sociological Review*, 14 (February, 1949), 1-11; Floyd Hunter, *Community Power Structure* (Chapel Hill: University of North Carolina Press, 1953); Ernest A. T. Barth and Baha Abu-Laban, "Power Structure and the Negro Sub-Community," *American Sociological Review*, 24 (February, 1959), 69-76.

the Middle South, it is a biracial community which is regarded here as a dual system with a supra-organization and structure. The Negro community is treated as a functional sub-community to be studied within a larger community aggregate, with organized ways, structure, and patterns of behavior that are distinct and yet a part of the larger whole.[3]

Relevant data are included for both whites and Negroes, but the investigation is designed as an intensive study of power and decision-making in the minority community as these relate to the dynamic issues of desegregation. Crescent City's sub-community has long been considered one of the more stable of its kind in the South—a mecca for a Negro middle class that numbers among its members leaders of national and international prominence. Well-established banking, insurance, and financial institutions; strongly organized voluntary associations; vocal political groups; stable family, educational, and religious institutions; and an industrial labor force characterize the city. It is, consequently, a community which offers some intriguing possibilities for the analysis of power and desegregation issues.

Perhaps the most controversial aspect of community power research today is the question of *how* to investigate and measure power. Most critics feel that measures of power have been too subjective. Certainly, until the reliability of various tools has been adequately tested, conclusions of power studies will be suspect. Although most social scientists would agree that we have, as yet, no wholly satisfactory method, there are those who argue in favor of the merits of one approach as opposed to another. And some few writers feel that a combination of methods might, at this stage of sophistication, prove most satisfactory. My sympathies accord with the latter group. It is my earnest

3. See Appendix A, Glossary, for the definition of "Community" and other concepts used throughout this study.

hope that the variety of methods I have employed to uncover the processes and structures involved in Crescent
City's race and power relations has eliminated some of the
pitfalls inherent in the use of a single approach.

From March, 1957, through February, 1960, I was
in and out of Crescent City—interviewing, observing, lis-
tening, and occasionally participating in sub-community
activities. The search for minority leaders was initiated
through the use of the power-attribution or reputation
method for identifying power elites. Modified forms of the
chain-referral technique were used with Negro and white
leaders. A stratified class sample of 283 respondents was
interviewed in the minority community, with the able assistance of two graduate students in anthropology.

Decision-making and policy formulation were analyzed
by tracing the actions of Negro and white leaders on five
specific issues. In addition to data gathered from extensive
interviews and from attendance at various committee and
organizational meetings, use was made of special documents, minutes of meetings, reports, speeches, policy statements and newspaper accounts (from March, 1957, through
April, 1960). The issues selected included desegregation
in schools and elsewhere; projects important to various institutional sectors of community life—economic, political,
civic, as well as legal and educational; and unique and re-
curring issues considered salient by both white and Negro
leaders, as well as sub-community informants.[4]

Attendance at church, school, and college functions,
dedication ceremonies for new sub-community facilities,
and other similar gatherings helped round out the picture,
filling in certain important details and providing me with
a keener appreciation of the sub-community's struggle for
a greater voice in community affairs.

4. For a more complete discussion of the methodology used in this
investigation, see Appendix B.

Three phenomena are central to our discussion of Crescent City—*power, desegregation,* and the *sub-community.* One implicit assumption in the work being done on community and national power is that there exists a limited amount of such power. An increase in the power of one group occurs at the expense of the power of another; conflict and struggle are inherent in all power relations. It is naïve to suggest the exclusion of conflict as a cardinal process in any study of power and race relations. Nevertheless, as Talcott Parsons and others have pointed out, it is fruitful to remember that power can also be viewed as an integrating factor—as a facility for performing a function on behalf of society. Thus power represents a capacity for mobilizing the resources of society for the attainment of goals to which a public commitment has been made.[5]

A second assumption in studies stressing conflict is that actions or decisions flow from the restricted interests of those who hold power. If one knows the group memberships of power leaders, one also knows who will profit most by their decisions. Another heuristic approach to the study of power, this one associated with David Truman and Seymour Lipset, views the *access* to power as a determining consideration. Here decisions made by those in the power structure are regarded as being determined in part by the influence other groups may have on these key decision-makers or by the consequences of the decisions themselves. To the extent that predictable reactions of any group to a decision will affect the direction of that decision, the group has access to the decision-making process.[6]

Access to power can be visualized in terms of political

5. Talcott Parsons, "The Distribution of Power in American Society," *World Politics,* 10 (October, 1957), 123-43.
6. Seymour M. Lipset, "Political Sociology," in *Sociology Today,* ed. R. K. Merton, L. Broom, and L. S. Cottrell, Jr. (New York: Basic Books, Inc., 1959), pp. 106-7; David Truman, *The Governmental Process* (New York: Alfred A. Knopf, 1955).

organization and voting power. The power of organized labor and of the working classes is greater than the number of their key decision-makers indicates. In Crescent City, specifically, no bond issue has much chance of passing without Negro support. While Negro leaders may not hold positions of power in the larger community, then, they nevertheless have access to this larger power through their power in the Negro community. The decisions of Negro leaders are, in turn, influenced by their followers and the voting population, who also have access to power.

It is true that deference is likely to be accorded the higher status group (business over labor; white over Negro), but power through the ballot gives the lower status group opportunity. And its influence can make itself felt even when no actual voting is involved, simply in terms of anticipated consequences.[7] That influence can be felt in many institutional areas of social life—legal, economic, educational, religious, as well as political. Furthermore, the legal sanctions of the 1954 Supreme Court decision on school desegregation have given additional strength to Negroes seeking access to power, beyond simple voting strength. The whole atmosphere of desegregation has served to redefine the demands of Negro leadership and to shape its actions.

Efforts of Negroes to secure access to power do involve conflict. Yet desegregation may be an example of a new goal for which the power resources of society must be deployed, and Negro power in this light functions on behalf of society. Power can thus be linked with both a conflict and a resource perspective. Both perspectives are included in the concept of "power" as used in this study, for I define

7. Truman, *The Governmental Process*, p. 262; Rupert B. Vance, "Freedom and Authority in the Social Structure," in *Freedom and Authority in our Times*, ed. L. Bryson *et al.* (New York Harper and Brothers [Published for the Conference on Science, Philosophy, and Religion], 1953), pp. 350-51.

power as the ability to induce others to take courses of action which they might not otherwise have taken.[8]

Power relations have been a favorite topic of social theorists for over two thousand years.[9] Yet that concept is in many respects as elusive today as it was when early philosophers wrote boldly of its meaning. One of many questions still plaguing students is where the precise locus of power is. Where do we turn for a study of power? Three approaches, early and recent, to the location of power may be cited. The first concerns power as it is located in the political structure; the second, the economic locus of power; and the third, which is a pluralistic doctrine, diffuse and various loci of power.

Historically, the analysis of power arose in the context

8. See Appendix A, Glossary. "Power" and "influence" will be used interchangeably here, as in many other studies. For a brief discussion of the conceptual differences, the reader is referred to the Glossary.

9. A number of recent studies concerned with power have been of valuable assistance throughout the present research. Those listed here are simply representative. Robert Agger, "Power Attributions in the Local Community: Theoretical and Research Considerations," *Social Forces,* 34 (May, 1956), 322-31; George Belknap and Ralph Smuckler, "Political Power Relations in a Midwestern City," *Public Opinion Quarterly,* 20 (Spring, 1956), 73-81; Herbert Kaufman and Victor Jones, "The Mystery of Power," *Public Administrative Review,* 14 (1954), 205-18; Robert Dahl, "Hierarchy Democracy, and Bargaining in Politics and Economics," in *Research Frontiers in Politics and Government* (Washington, D. C.: Brookings Institution, 1955), pp. 50-57; Harry M. Scoble, "Yankeetown: Leadership in Three Decision Making Processes" (Mimeographed paper read at the meeting of the American Political Science Association, Washington, D. C., September, 1956); Nelson W. Polsby, "The Sociology of Community Power: A Reassessment," *Social Forces,* 37 (March, 1959), 232-34; *ibid.,* "Three Problems in Community Power Analysis," *American Sociological Review,* 24 (December, 1959), 796-803; Hunter, *Community Power Structure;* Delbert C. Miller, "Industry and Community Power Structure: A Comparative Study of an American and an English City," *American Sociological Review,* 23 (February, 1958), 9-15; Roland Pellegrin and Charles H. Coates, "Absentee-Owned Corporations and Community Power Structures," *American Journal of Sociology,* LXI (March, 1956), 413-19; Robert O. Schulze, "The Role of Economic Dominants in Community Power Structure," *American Sociological Review,* 23 (February, 1958), 3-9.

of man's political institutions. Its primary basis and ultimate locus were seen as the government or state. From
Aristotle to Machiavelli, power was regarded as a function
of political control. Hobbes expounded the need of the
masses to be ruled. And the recent work of many political
scientists, such as Robert Dahl, Robert Agger, George
Belknap, Harry Scoble, Nelson W. Polsby, and others, is
primarily concerned with power as it is "personified" in the
political structure of a social system. Failure to realize
that power can be located in many centers has, however,
confused the theoretical understanding of power and re-
tarded inquiry into the conditions and consequences of its
exercise. Political authority is a genuine form of power,
but it is one form, not the only form, as R. H. Tawney, the
English social historian, has so ably observed.[10]

The writings of Marx stimulated a shifting of sights
regarding the locus of power. For Marx wealth and power
were practically synonymous. So wide was his influence
that today the concept of economic power is often accepted
without analysis and without reservation. There are those,
however, who feel that dominance of economic institutions
in capitalist societies results not so much from the inevitable
character of economic institutions as from the character of
capitalism itself. In this view, it is because capitalism rests
on a class structure deriving basically from economic interests and power that it has been possible for economic
institutions to determine so largely the other institutions, to
enjoy the advantage of superior status which makes possible
easier access to the positions of power.[11]

Many recent studies of community and national power

10. R. H. Tawney, *Equality* (London: Allen and Unwin, Ltd., 1929),
pp. 228-30.
11. Robert S. Lynd, "Power in American Society as Resource and
Problem," in *Problems of Power in American Democracy,* ed. Arthur
Kornhauser (Detroit: Wayne State University Press, 1957), pp. 24-25;
Truman, *The Governmental Process,* pp. 253-60.

have stressed the economic dominants in the power structure. Mills suggests that the power of the "very rich" and the "corporate rich" is great and by virtue of cumulative advantage is becoming greater. Floyd Hunter, Delbert Miller, Roland Pellegrin, Charles Coates, Robert Schulze, and others have found the business, industrial, and financial world to be supplying the top power figures. Whether this is a reflection of bias, the influence of the Marxist position, or a flaw in methodology, or whether it is the actual result of the structure of the American capitalist society has yet to be conclusively determined. There have been several strong criticisms of the extreme importance approaches of this kind accord economic power.

Economically conditioned power, according to Max Weber in his classic critique of Marx, is not identical with power as such. Rather, the emergence of economic power may be the consequence of the existence of other kinds of power.[12] To deny the self-sufficiency of economic power, Harold Lasswell and Abraham Kaplan suggest, is not to regard all forms of power as being always of equal importance. Nor is it to deny the importance economic power has had. But to say that wealth does serve as a power base is far from saying that economic power is the only form of power or always the most fundamental.[13] Tawney expresses somewhat the same notion when he asserts that all forms of power are not in the last resort economic, for men desire other than temporal goals and fear other than economic evils, even though most forms of power have some economic roots.[14] Concentrated economic power does not always have its way, as is evident in the rise of the labor

12. Max Weber, "Class, Status, Party," in *From Max Weber: Essays in Sociology,* trans. and ed. H. H. Gerth and C. Wright Mills (New York: Oxford University Press, 1946), pp. 180-81.

13. Harold D. Lasswell and Abraham Kaplan, *Power and Society* (New Haven: Yale University Press, 1950), p. 497.

14. Tawney, *Equality,* p. 230.

movement and legislative and governmental control of business.

Recently a number of writers, perhaps as a gesture of rejection of both political reductionism and Marxian determinism, have been stressing the great diffusion that has occurred in power relations in our society. The pluralistic thesis in its more extreme form suggests that there are no dominant power centers, no concentrations of influence. It holds that power is so scattered, shared by so many diverse groups "which combine, break, federate, and form coalitions and constellations of power in a flux of restless alterations," that none is in a position to make decisions favorable to itself. Power, being mercurial, resists the attraction to locate. Thus the locus of power in society is almost undiscoverable.[15] Whether this thesis is exaggerated remains to be seen, but studies to date do not support it.

Neither a monistic interpretation nor a diffuse and pluralistic interpretation of power centers seems sufficient to explain the location of power. First of all, power is a social phenomenon. We speak of a social power of which economic, political, religious, scientific, personal, and mili-

15. Earl Latham, *The Group Basis of Politics* (Ithaca: Cornell University Press, 1952), pp. 49-50; David Riesman, "Who Has the Power," in *Class Status and Power,* ed. R. Bendix and S. Lipset (Glencoe, Illinois: The Free Press, 1953), p. 26. A somewhat subdued and more acceptable statement of the pluralistic thesis is found in de Gré's discussion of the "pluralistic society" which he characterizes as consisting of large, well-integrated groups representing divisions of interests and values. The power of these groups is limited by the necessity of taking into account the interests of other groups. Gerard De Gré, "Freedom and Social Structure," in *Sociological Analysis,* ed. Logan Wilson and William Kolb (New York: Harcourt, Brace and Co., 1949), pp. 528-29. Because a consensus must exist among the various groups concerning the desirability and validity of the underlying institutional structure, no society has achieved an optimum degree of pluralist organization, according to De Gré. Too, the fact that formally separate interest groups trade back and forth in terms of their respective power does not indicate that this trading is either voluntary or equal or that some groups or institutions are not dependent upon others. See Lynd, "Power in American Society," *Problems of Power,* p. 30.

tary power are some of the various aspects. The primitive
base and ultimate locus of power, then, as R. M. MacIver
has emphasized, are to be sought in society and community,
not in government or the state or any other specific institutional structure.[16]

Second, we say that, though power is expressed in social
institutions (those persistent systems of behavior that have
developed within a given society to serve certain needs
regarded as essential for survival of the group), it is not
primarily autonomous but derives from the social *structure*.
Social structure consists of relatively fixed, persistent, and
functionally interrelated units or elements of a social group
or social system—institutions, social classes, associations,
power and leadership groupings, racial and ethnic groups,
or other enduring social units. So power relations reflect
the social structure of which institutions and other such
units are a part.

It must be remembered, of course, that social structure,
as well as institutions and power, is an abstraction, not to
be reified. It is predicated of people and organizations concerned with durable interests and behaving in relation to the
basic values and norms of a given group or society. Power
is a relation among people, not something external to this
relation. One cannot therefore concentrate on institutions
or structures per se but must look further at social *processes*
—the characteristic way interaction occurs—by focusing
on individual and group behavior as reflected in the institutional, associational, or class structure. Moreover, while
power may rest on various bases or resources—wealth,
property, prestige, status, office, or function—these bases
are not themselves power unless they are utilized in organized association with one another.

And so we turn to the community as the social unit

16. R. M. MacIver, *Web of Government* (New York: The Macmillan Co., 1947), p. 193.

small enough for observation of majority-minority power relations.

Community power studies have been criticized for their reliance exclusively on structure and consequent lack of attention to the dynamic processes of decision-making. In the research described in this book, however, the decisions associated with the broad issue of desegregation have been used as a window from which to view leadership and power in action.

We need to observe behavior involved in power, rather than relying solely on intentions or reputations. In this way we can learn whether there is a single structure of power or several; whether decision-makers remain the same from issue to issue; whether leaders are monolithic in terms of desires, goals, and values; and what the breadth and kinds of decisions are that are made at the hands of various power figures. Moreover, a focus on decisions may enable us to observe more accurately the kinds of roles played and functions performed by the power leaders—obtaining consent, enacting new projects, suppressing issues, fighting new proposals, raising money, or lending prestige.[17]

Desegregation is the result of basic changes in the social system. The obvious legal changes of the past decade come to mind, but other changes, less dramatic and frequently unnoticed, have had their part in weakening the foundations of segregation. Shifts in the economy, demographic alterations, and increased mechanization, urbanization, industrialization, migration, and political participation have all wrought changes in Negro-white relations.[18] The

17. See Peter H. Rossi, "Community Decision Making," *Administrative Science Quarterly,* 1 (March, 1957), 415-41; Nelson W. Polsby, "The Sociology of Community Power: A Reassessment," *Social Forces,* 37 (March, 1959), 232-36.
18. George E. Simpson and J. Milton Yinger, "The Sociology of Race and Ethnic Relations," in *Sociology Today,* ed. R. K. Merton, L.

Court school desegregation decision, for that matter, has engendered changes going quite beyond the limited degree of its actual implementation. So while we may be concerned in part with issues arising as a result of the 1954 Court ruling, it becomes apparent that the whole issue of desegregation is much wider than those aspects of it explicitly related to litigation for admitting Negro children into heretofore all-white schools. It is an issue affording the Negro leader a weapon cutting across many institutional sectors. He can be expected to view a wide variety of current community problems in terms of the new patterns being set by these shifts in basic institutional structures, as well as by changes in the "law of the land." For these reasons, the study of local community policy and decision-making relative to desegregation can do much to illuminate the nature of the power system.[19]

Although I am aware that no complete understanding of Negro leadership and power—or of desegregation in a given community—is possible without an analysis of white leadership, the white community is not my primary concern. Data pertinent to the research have been collected from white leaders and will be analyzed. It is to the subcommunity life and leaders, however, that I shall direct the

Broom, and L. S. Cottrell, Jr. (New York: Basic Books, Inc., 1959), pp. 384-94. The usefulness of the concepts found in structure-function theory is just beginning to be tested in work on race relations and holds some promise for the understanding of such issues as desegregation.
  19. See Robin M. Williams, Jr., Burton Fisher, and Irving Janis, "Educational Desegregation as a Context for Basic Social Science Research," *American Sociological Review*, 21 (October, 1956), 577-88. See also E. A. T. Barth and S. D. Johnson, "Community Power and a Typology of Social Issues," *Social Forces*, 38 (October, 1959), 29-30. The authors have attempted to point out the importance of *types of issues* under consideration by decision-makers and to develop the basis for a typology of such issues. Their discussion is of interest to me since it would seem to indicate that the issues selected for study here are perhaps broader and more inclusive than might be gathered from the fact that they revolve around desegregation. See chapter v.

major share of my attention. Research efforts in power relations, with but few exceptions, have concentrated on the white segment of the biracial community. There exist, as a consequence, many outright assumptions regarding the aims and actions of Negroes and Negro leaders, with much of the thinking both contradictory and confusing.

The Negro community is not a homogeneous unit. Like its white counterpart, it has lines of differentiation based on socio-economic variation, religious preference,. length of residence, ideological convictions, and racial militancy—to mention a few. But while there is considerable diversity among Negro communities, the response of the minority community to desegregation depends largely upon the quality of organization and leadership to be found in it.

Furthermore, the degree of community racial integration that is eventually achieved will depend in large part upon the roles played by both minority and majority leaders. The process of integration across group lines involves the values, traditions, and behavior patterns of both groups. Because of barriers in communication, one race often does not know the core values or aspirations of the other. It seems important, therefore, that some community studies of power and desegregation focus upon the Negro community. What kinds of communication and interaction are present within the minority community? How do internal differentiations affect attitudes toward leadership, power, and issues such as desegregation, and the actions growing out of these? What changes have occurred in the relationships between Negro and white leaders in arriving at decisions in which race issues are or are not involved? Have the court decisions appreciably changed old communication channels, old majority-minority interaction patterns? In short, can we see a new struggle for power in the way Negroes now deal with issues?

We should also be concerned with changes in the type of Negro leader now active. Myrdal found that Negro leadership has always been related to the pattern of race relations in the United States, both with respect to time and place. Is there now emerging a functional leader in the Negro community, as Frazier hints, or is the "race leader" still typical?[20]   And how does the nature of leadership affect the power structure? And in turn, how has the whole issue of desegregation affected the various types of leaders one would expect to find in a minority community? These are some of the questions and considerations that have led to this study of the Negro community and power structure.[21]

20. Gunnar Myrdal, *An American Dilemma* (New York: Harper and Brothers, 1944), pp. 709-80; E. Franklin Frazier, *The Negro in the United States* (New York: The Macmillan Co., 1949), pp. 548-63.

21. For a list of working hypotheses used in the study, see Appendix B.

CHAPTER II

THE SETTING OF BIRACIAL POWER

CRESCENT CITY is part of an emerging polynucleated area forming an industrial crescent extending roughly from southern Virginia to northern Georgia.[1] A small Piedmont town of 7000 people in 1900, it had reached an estimated population of 80,000 by 1960, approximately 35 per cent of which was Negro. Both the white and Negro population have continued to increase, but the percentage of the Negro population to the white population has been declining since 1940, in keeping with the regional trend of outward migration among southern Negroes.

Beginning as a way station along the old Mid-South State Railway, the original town developed around the rapidly growing tobacco and textile industries of the area. A factory for tobacco manufacturing was founded in the 1850's. Following the Civil War, textile plants were established. The small community at first grew from north to south along the railroad lines, later expanding to the east and west with the development of new factories, warehouses, railroads, and highways. Residential areas developed on the fringes of the central business district and

1. See Ralph W. Pfouts, "Economic Interrelations Between Cities in the Piedmont," *Research Previews* (Institute for Research in Social Science, University of North Carolina), 6 (March, 1959). Piedmont boundaries as quoted by various authors vary slightly depending upon the subjects of their studies.

in a radial direction along the ridges and main transportation routes.

Today there is a concentration of industrial, wholesale, and commercial areas in the center of the city and along the main lines of transportation. Railroads divide the community into pie-shaped sectors. Major thoroughfares and United States highways converging in the city have also tended to divide it, as industrial and commercial activities have become distributed along them. Most residential development follows a radial pattern along the thoroughfares leading from Crescent City, with some mixed commercial and residential use still to be found along the fringe areas of the central business district. In recent years residential expansion has occurred in outlying suburban areas and the valleys beyond the suburbs. Negro neighborhoods, varying in size from four to five blocks to several hundred blocks, are dispersed like pockets throughout the city's residential area.

Present-day Crescent City is a manufacturing and retail-trade center of some importance. By 1958 there were 125 industries manufacturing a wide variety of goods including asphalt, cement, cigarettes, containers, fertilizers, furniture, hosiery, livestock feed, machinery, mattresses, motors, precision instruments, sheets, and yarn. Of these, the most important are still the textile and tobacco industries, now absentee owned.

Although the community is one of the top manufacturing centers in Mid-South State, its share of manufacturing activity in the region has declined since 1940. Wholesale sales, business receipts, and retail sales have also shown a decline. The city is retaining a smaller share each year of the dollar-value of business in the Greater Piedmont Crescent. Another fact affecting the economic make-up of the city is the lack of diversity in employment distribution. Fully 30 per cent of the working population is concentrated in manufacturing, primarily tobacco and cotton textiles. A study of industrial diversification revealed that in 1955 Crescent City was one of the ten most specialized of 127 United States cities in which research was conducted.[2] It would seem, then, that Crescent City's economic future depends on its very few major industries and their markets.

The per-capita income of the community was $1200 in 1950, $150 below the national average, although $220 above Mid-South State's average. The median income of the Crescent City Negro was $1000, compared to $1900 for whites in 1950. Wages are increasing at a rate considerably below that in other urbanized centers in the Piedmont Crescent.[3]

The none too satisfactory economic situation of Crescent City is of concern to many of the leaders of both the white and Negro communities. Many informants have suggested that the community will "wither on the economic vine" unless something can be done to rejuvenate the economic base. In an effort to offset the trend, committees have been formed and projects undertaken by the more progressive leaders in the hope of attracting new industries and commercial enterprises.

The community has a city manager and an elected City Council presided over by a mayor. It is the Council that seems to have the ultimate authority to govern the community. The Council is made up of Crescent City business and professional men almost exclusively. Two or three of the city's most influential leaders are usually "called" to serve. Sometimes young white businessmen use the City Council as a steppingstone. Occasionally a faculty member from one of the two white universities in the city is elected

2. Alan Rogers, "Some Aspects of Industrial Diversification in the United States," *Papers and Proceedings of the Regional Science Association,* I (State College: Pennsylvania State University, 1955), B1-B15.
3. United States Census Bureau, *Seventeenth Census of the United States,* II (Washington: U. S. Government Printing Office, 1950).

to serve on the Council. Labor has been represented, but not in recent years. Negroes have had a representative on the Council since 1953.

The mayor, a Catholic, is the owner of a large retail furniture and appliance center with branches in other towns. He seems to wield a significant influence in economic, civic, and political matters and has had labor and Negro support for the past several years. The city manager is responsible for carrying out policy and for running the local bureaucracy.

A listing of "vital statistics" or a brief ecological description cannot, of course, provide a real feeling of a community. As Robert Park points out, a city is more than a physical mechanism, a geographical, ecological, political, or economic unit. It is also a state of mind, a body of customs and traditions, and the organized attitudes and sentiments inherent in these customs.[4] As one talks with the citizens of Crescent City, a picture takes form. Crescent has neither the ways of a big metropolitan center with cosmopolitan airs nor the ways of a small town with its open neighborliness and inquisitiveness. Crescent City lies somewhere in between. One almost feels that the city is striving to find itself, trying to decide what direction it should take. The citizens seem to have mixed feelings about their town. One can sense a certain amount of pride as a result of the community's growing reputation as an educational center. Three colleges and universities, a fine medical foundation, and a new creative-art center have gained national attention. And these basic organizations are coming to have a quiet, uplifting influence on the community as a whole. But in other areas of community life there seems to be a paucity of pride. Some white informants lament the lack of community spirit and leader-

4. Robert Park, E. W. Burgess, and R. D. McKenzie, *The City* (Chicago: University of Chicago Press, 1925), pp. 1-25.

ship.   They look with envy to neighboring cities and compare Crescent City unfavorably.   "Elizabeth has shopping
centers that are far superior.   Brownsville has a fine, for-
ward-looking leadership that really knows how to get things
done."   One white respondent said, "We are supposed to
be proud of Crescent City, but no one tells us what to be
proud of.   Leaders take no stand on community problems.
They act as though by being silent about them, problems
will just disappear.   Race problems, economic development, city planning—they treat them all the same—do
nothing, say nothing."   To be sure, such sentiments do not
express the feelings of all of the city's citizens.   But when
one hears similar refrains over and over among whites and
Negroes alike, they cannot be ignored.   The tenor of Crescent City as a community, after all, will have a bearing
on community power.   And surely it will have a bearing on
such issues as desegregation.

    Crescent City's Negro citizens are located in five resi-
dential areas.   With a few notable exceptions these sections are characterized by deficiencies usually found in
minority areas—sub-standard housing with a highly concentrated population, scant water and sewage facilities,
unpaved streets and infrequent street lights, a few run-down
neighborhood business establishments, and few or no recreation facilities.

    Holis district, roughly three times larger than all other
Negro sections together, is the hub of the sub-community
life.   It begins on the northwest side of Crescent City, hug-
ging the rail and highway routes at the edge of the commercial and wholesale areas.   It fans out along the flat-
lands, moving upward and outward along the ridges and
hills of outlying areas.   At the extreme western end of
Holis is the University Park area.   This is the Negro upper-
class district.   The Negro college, hospital, and civic and

recreation centers, and the largest Negro churches, are found in University Park. Attractive brick and clapboard houses face the paved, tree-lined streets. Landscaped yards and two-car garages give the area a look of prosperity. It is the home of the successful Negro professional and businessman.

While Holis represents the heart of the Negro community, there is, nevertheless, strong neighborhood spirit to be found in two or three of the smaller Negro sections of town. Dayton, for example, a small area of not more than eight or nine blocks located in the southern part of the city, has an active and loyal group of citizens. They have their own unofficial council that has worked tirelessly to instill in residents a sense of pride in the appearance of their neighborhood and to obtain a modern recreation center, paved streets, and adequate lighting. Yet the residents here, like those of other sections, look to Holis when the issues are drawn between Negro and white. Before the white community, the sub-community tries very hard to present a united front.

The largest Negro business and financial firms are located in substantial, well-kept office buildings just off the main thoroughfare in the heart of Crescent City's business district. The larger concerns have from time to time in recent years purchased additional property in this vicinity and elsewhere, as part of a modest expansion program. The main Negro business district, however, is located in Holis, beginning along Potter Street, which runs parallel to north-south transportation routes cutting through the city. It moves up Folsom Avenue, a main thoroughfare bisecting Holis in an easterly direction. For the most part, the business district is made up of small, drab, unkempt shops—grocery stores, lunch rooms, cleaning establishments, shoe-shine shops, and beauty parlors. As one moves up Folsom Avenue toward the crest of the hill, the establishments become more substantial. There are branch offices of the main banks, real estate offices, insurance agencies, undertaking establishments and a few professional offices for doctors, dentists, and lawyers.

Crescent City very early attracted Negroes, and over the years they built its now small but nevertheless impressive number of Negro banking, real estate, commercial, and insurance firms. Relatively, of course, Negro business is modest when compared broadly with business in the white world. Even when they are most successful, Negro firms actually are small-scale operations. In the context of Crescent City, however, Negro business is significant. As one white informant, the president of the largest home-owned white corporation, said, "Why, the Negroes have the largest home-owned firm in town, with assets over $65,000,000. Our own assets are only $47,000,000. Of course the absentee-owned tobacco and textile factories and the Whitehead Bank are larger, but for home-owned operations, we can't beat those Negro concerns." It is apparent that the economic structure of the Negro sub-community is one vitally important factor in the understanding of the power structure of the greater biracial community.

As Hylan Lewis observed of the Negro community of "Kent," the sub-community of Crescent City is a functional sub-system within the whole metropolis, supplying much of the labor force which makes the wheels of Crescent City at large operate.[5] But it is also in many respects an isolated community, with its own organized ways, patterns of behavior, and structure, although this isolation has been modified slowly over the years.

5. Hylan Lewis, *Blackways of Kent* (Chapel Hill: University of North Carolina Press, 1953).

CHAPTER III

ORGANIZATION AND STRUCTURE IN THE CRESCENT NEGRO COMMUNITY

THOUGH power derives from the social structure of the community, the concept of social structure fails to convey a proper sense of the dynamic and developing nature of social relationships. We can view social *structure* as an abstraction derived from the observed patterns of the social organization. Social *organization,* on the other hand, can be defined as the totality of these continuing social relationships[1]—the complex and dynamic interplay of institutions and people.

The concept of structure does satisfy the need for a method of demonstrating the formal relationships among the parts of a society or community. John Bennett and Melvin Tumin see structure as consisting of (1) the statuses or positions people occupy, (2) groups or clusters of such statuses, and (3) institutions or larger systems of interrelated groups serving the basic needs of society.[2] Their approach resembles that of Parsons, who believes that the social structure can be operationally defined in terms of institutionalized patterns—of social institutions and associations, as well as of social differentiation and stratification.[3]

1. Gordon W. Blackwell, "A Theoretical Framework for Sociological Research in Community Organization," *Social Forces,* 33 (October, 1954), 57-64.

2. John Bennett and Melvin Tumin, *Social Life* (New York: Alfred A. Knopf, 1949), pp. 70-73.

3. Talcott Parsons, *Essays in Sociological Theory, Pure and Applied*

To understand leadership in Crescent City's Negro community, I began by examining the social organization from which the social structure could be abstracted. Merton favored this approach when he observed that, in order to keep from overlooking the role of power in society, it is necessary to consider systematically the specific groups supporting given social institutions and the interpersonal influences of these groups in the community.[4] Furthermore, in Robin Williams' view it is also necessary to be concerned with possible interrelationships between institutions and between other social groupings, since they are not completely autonomous systems. To investigate power properly, then, we must attend to the web of relationships between groups.[5]

Accordingly, we will initiate our leadership analysis by observing pertinent characteristics of the class system, of the major institutional systems, and of some of the individuals or groups whose roles, within basic groupings, are basic to the sub-community. All the names employed to identify individuals are fictitious. To insure anonymity, in some instances position in the social structure and biographical details have also been altered. Despite these modifications, however, every effort has been made to preserve the essential dynamics and the reality of the community. The aim is, if not perfect veracity, perfect verisimilitude.

The Warner class-caste model of stratification in the biracial South has been a basic point of departure for many students of race relations. Something like a class-caste sys-

(Glencoe, Illinois: The Free Press, 1945), p. 163; Blackwell, "A Theoretical Framework," pp. 60-61.

4. Robert Merton, Discussion of papers by Talcott Parsons, *American Sociological Review*, 13 (April, 1948), 165-68.

5. Robert M. Williams, Jr., *American Society* (New York: Alfred A. Knopf, 1951), pp. 443-44, 504-6.

CRESCENT CITY

WHITE   NEGRO

Upper
  Financial, Industrial Execu-
    utives
  Large-Business Owners-Man-
    agers
  Professionals
    Doctors
    Corporation Lawyers
    Top University Adminis-
      trators

                                    Upper
                                      Financial, Insurance, Real
                                        Estate Executives
                                      Professionals
                                        Doctors
                                        Corporation Lawyers
                                        College Administrators
                                          and Faculty-Members
                                      Large-Business and Com-
                                        mercial Owners-Man-
                                        agers

Middle
  Business Proprietors
  Professionals
    University Faculty Mem-
      bers
    Teachers
    Ministers
    Social Service Workers
  White Collar Workers
  Skilled Workers

                                    Middle
                                      Small-Business Proprietors
                                      Professionals
                                        Lower-Rank College Fac-
                                          ulty Members, Lawyers
                                          in Private Practice
                                        Teachers
                                        Ministers
                                        Social Service Workers
                                      White Collar Workers
                                      Skilled and Service Workers
                                      Semi-skilled Workers

Lower
  Semi-skilled Workers
  Unskilled Laborers
  Unemployed
  Illegal

                                    Lower
                                      Domestic and Other Servants
                                      Unskilled Laborers
                                      Unemployed
                                      Illegal

Fig. 1. Class structure of Crescent City, 1960.

tem existed in Crescent City until the early 1900's, when the stratification pattern started to change. Caste barriers began to give way in many areas, though first in the economic field. Negro education broadened; gradually some occupational doors opened; labor unions established joint councils;

church boards on the local and state level began to hold
integrated meetings; Negro representation appeared on community service committees; Negroes were appointed to
politically controlled committees and commissions. Negro
voting increased. Slowly the legal foundation for segregation in buses, recreation areas, and schools began to crum-
ble. The old patterns of race relations shifted steadily toward equalitarianism.

In individual communities, of course, change is gradual,
and Crescent City is no exception. It would be misleading
to say that racial barriers have disappeared, or that Negroes
are free to move within the community on the basis of
equality with whites. But change is occurring, and with
increasing rapidity. The caste-like structure, now in a
state of transition, is giving way to a dual-class system,
and there are increasing contacts between class equals
across color lines. This phenomenon may be occurring in
other parts of the South as well, as a study in the New
Orleans Negro community reveals.[6]

The class structure of Crescent City (Fig. 1) can be
roughly diagrammed to include three broad classes. In the
Negro sub-community, it might have been possible to distinguish among four classes—upper, upper middle, lower
middle, and lower—as Warner did in Chicago.[7] Such

6. J. H. Rohrer and M. S. Edmonson, *The Eighth Generation* (New
York: Harper and Brothers, 1959), pp. 12-28. This work was designed
as a follow-up study of Allison Davis and John Dollard, *Children of
Bondage* (Washington: American Council on Education, 1940).

7. W. Lloyd Warner, B. H. Junker, and W. A. Adams, *Color and
Human Nature* (Washington: American Council on Education, 1941),
pp. 20-23. It is as yet early to tell, but there is some indication that a
fourth class group, the upper-middle, may be emerging. This group is
still too small to be considered a class. It is a fluid aggregate between
the upper and middle classes, with some difference in norms and values.
The social behavior of the group suggests that it may represent what
Frazier has described as the new "black bourgeoisie." Members of the
group are often "newcomers" to the community. Their education and
occupational positions are similar to those of the upper class, but their
value patterns are at variance to the older upper class traditions of

finer distinctions, however, serve mainly to indicate the fluid nature of class in the changing sub-community. The class structure of the sub-community is, indeed, flexible. There is no clear line between upper and middle classes or between middle and lower classes. Social mobility is apparent. However, by defining class operationally in terms of income, occupation, education, religion, and other social factors, and by taking into account an apparent variation in certain basic values and goals, it was possible to differentiate with some exactness the three broad categories mentioned above.

E. Franklin Frazier contends that the Negro upper class retains its status mainly because of segregation. If members of the Negro upper class were integrated into the total society, he believes that their occupations, income, and values would place them in the middle class.[8] Frazier's position is well supported by evidence from various parts of the United States. In some respects, however, Crescent City's Negro class structure is an exception to Frazier's observation. Slavery was not a dominant part of the early social structure; the largest number of slaves owned by one man (he was a farmer) in the area that now comprises Crescent and two adjacent counties is recorded as twenty-four. Perhaps fifty other individuals and families had slaves, ranging in numbers from one to ten. The first Negro resident, a slave, nevertheless operated the only local blacksmith shop.

Not until the end of the Civil War did the community begin to expand. Many of the present upper-class families of both racial groups date from this period. Of the white

---

Crescent City, as well as to the Protestant ethic of the middle class. They are considered social "strainers" and are not really accepted by the upper-class families. See E. Franklin Frazier, *Black Bourgeoisie* (Glencoe, Illinois: The Free Press, 1957).

8. E. Franklin Frazier, *The Negro in the United States* (New York: The Macmillan Co., 1949), p. 291.

upper class, only the Lords, the Humbolts, and the Corts can claim residence in the area prior to 1865. Others of the white elite—the Whitneys, the Vales, the Pearsons, and the Crawfords—established themselves in the period following the war. Many more came in the late 1800's and early 1900's, just as did the ancestors of the individuals that now comprise the Negro community's economic and prestige dominants.

In the Negro community, then, most of the immigrants who arrived by the end of the Civil War were freedmen, many of them free mulattoes. "Industrious and thrifty citizens," they purchased land and developed small businesses and manufacturing concerns or worked as skilled artisans. This group—including the Nelsons, the Pattersons, the Conners, the Whitings, and the Arthurs—were followed by physicians, teachers, pharmacists, barbers, and small entrepreneurs. All were proud of their genteel tradition, which was based upon the morals and manners of the white aristocracy. Many had obtained an education unusual for their time. Others with little formal education proved to be astute and able leaders. Following these initial immigrants came the Marcys, the Alders, the Martins, the Knights, the Warners, the Stoddards, and the Swansons, who joined some of the earlier residents to become the economic elite.

With money earned from real estate and business investments, these families combined resources to develop somewhat larger business establishments—insurance, banking, savings and loan, mortgage, surety and bonding, brokerage, and real estate companies, and small manufacturing concerns such as brick-making enterprises. Many of the members of these families were physicians, ministers, and teachers, as well as businessmen.

Inspired as the founders of these enterprises were by the spirit of modern capitalism, they also exhibited the old-fashioned virtues, striving to attain respectability through industry and morality. They remained frugal and abstemious in their habits. Many of the upper-class members of the sub-community today are direct descendants—children, grandchildren, and great-grandchildren—of these early pioneers. Through the years, they have held positions of responsibility and authority in business and have conformed to the traditions of the genteel class.

The numbers of the Negro upper class have been swelled by socially mobile newcomers. Some of them were members of prominent Negro families elsewhere. Higher-education and status-occupations provided the avenue of entry for others. Intermarriage consolidated the new families with the old into a single group. It should be emphasized, when we speak of "swelling numbers," that the Negro upper class of Crescent City is small, consisting of probably no more than 5 per cent of the sub-community. In this, the Crescent sub-community corresponds to the general distribution of the Negro upper class at large.

Perhaps the most important distinction between the two upper classes, Negro and white, is the broader economic base of the white elite. This distinction, which extends to the lower levels of the social structure, was represented in Fig. 1 by staggering the two class structures. Nevertheless, in Crescent City the two upper classes are otherwise rather strikingly similar.

The upper-class families are small—one-, two-, and occasionally three-child families. The children are taught the responsibilities of their position early and what these entail in terms of behavior and goals. They are encouraged to cultivate friends from families whose status and prestige are similar to their own. Courtesy to all classes, Negro and white, is required, but the children are not trained to behave in a subservient fashion to whites. Respect for and fidelity to the family name and pride in the accomplishments of the extended kin group are stressed. Children of the wealthier families attend private schools or the public schools in upper-class neighborhoods. All such families strive to send their sons and daughters to the better colleges in the North or the best private Negro colleges and then to professional or graduate school.

Members of the Negro upper class attend the prominent Negro Protestant churches and serve on their highest lay governing bodies, rarely at subordinate levels. Prominent as leaders of a variety of community agencies, they add prestige to such organizations. Many believe they have a responsibility for the whole community and consequently do not tend to draw class distinctions, particularly in business, political, and civic affairs.

The social life of the Negro upper class is dominated by the families of the business executives, the doctors, and the upper echelons of the college faculty and administration. Some of those especially active in social affairs are wives of the sub-community leaders—Mrs. Silas Alder, Mrs. R. E. Laroux, Mrs. Nathan Banks, Mrs. M. Conners, and Mrs. William Patterson III—but many are wives of men who hold prestige positions in the sub-community but who take little active part in community affairs. The wives of physicians play an especially active social role.

The social life of the Negro upper class has largely been a private affair—small bridge clubs of the prominent professional and business men and their wives, private parties held in the home and not given press notice. There are in Crescent City, however, two chapters of national Negro social organizations. The Jack and Jill Club is made up of parents and children of the high-status group and provides "proper social contacts" for upper-class youth. Very recently, a social club known as the Links organized a chapter in the city. It, too, is an upper-class group; its membership, like that of the Jack and Jill Club, is restricted to the elite. In fact, membership of the two organizations tends to overlap, with most of the members of both coming from the younger upper-class families, with a small number of the so-called "social strainers," who are not accepted fully by the upper class, also participating.

One informant explains the new Links chapter as an unfortunate intrusion by a national group of extravagantly social-minded Negroes who want to exploit the "prestige market" in Crescent. He shares many of Frazier's views with regard to the new Black Bourgeoisie and is hopeful that his community can remain as aloof from this value-orientation as possible. If not, he fears that the families whose values and norms have made the Crescent City Negro upper class unique will gradually yield to the "Negro Babbitts" that are common in other areas. He observes that in recent years a group involved in the "poker cycle" described by Frazier[9] appeared in Crescent City. The group was composed of four or five "social strainers" hovering on the edges of the upper class. There is concern that the younger generation will become enamoured of such activities.

The Wednesday Luncheon Club, made up of business and professional men, meets weekly at the Negro Y.M.C.A. Although it is largely a social organization, it affords the opportunity for informal contacts on the policy- and decision-making level. The economic dominants meet regularly for lunch in the Beta Dining Room, which is owned and supported by the insurance and banking firms. It, too, serves as an informal focus for the policy- and decision-making groups. The Greek-letter fraternities also play a part in the social life, especially for the younger upper-class members. The Natchez Tennis Club, where the Crescent Negro Council and other Negro groups meet regularly, is another social focus.

9. Frazier, *Black Bourgeoisie*, pp. 211-13, 220-22.

In many community class structures there is an overlap of characteristics between the upper- and middle-class Negroes. Crescent City is no exception. Some of the values of the two classes are similar; educational and occupational aspirations overlap for some; so also do family patterns and religious affiliations. Perhaps the most significant differentiation between the two strata derives from the traditions of the old, prestige families. Their inherited status and positions in the economic institutions, the pattern of following the father's profession, and endogamy identify this group. There is a keen awareness of the family past and a strong effort to preserve its genteel and moral traditions for future generations.

The Negro middle class in Crescent City, like the upper class, is based on relatively stable marriage. The economic dominance of the husband is the ideal, although it does not always actually obtain. Children are rigidly disciplined, and strict adherence is practiced to the Protestant ethic of morality and thrift. In occupation and education, the middle class is much more heterogenous than the upper class. Some members are professionals—college or public school teachers, some lawyers, ministers, social service workers, funeral directors or embalmers. More are white-collar workers, skilled and service workers, and, occasionally, semi-skilled persons with steady jobs. Wives are often employed. They are teachers, nurses, beauticians, clerks, stenographers, elevator operators, and skilled or semi-skilled and service workers.

Roughly 55 to 60 per cent of the middle-class families own their homes, compared to approximately 95 per cent of the upper-class families and only 8 or 9 per cent of the lower-class families. Most of the members of the middle class have completed high school, and about 20 to 25 per cent have attended college. Some share church affiliations with the upper class, and some attend fundamentalist churches in lower-class neighborhoods. Most, however, are staunch communicants of the Baptist, Methodist, and "African" churches, all middle-class. They are eager to have their children complete high school and obtain college or vocational training. Families tend to be small, with few having as many as four or five children. Children participate in the Boy and Girl Scouts, summer recreation programs, and Y.M.- and Y.W.C.A. activities. Adult social life centers around garden clubs, sewing clubs, and other similar social and literary groups. Lodges and fraternal orders—the Elks, the Masons, and the Knights of Solomon —include among their membership a cross section of middle and lower classes, but leadership is usually drawn from the middle class. The same is true of the veterans' organizations. Church guilds and the P.T.A. are also important social and service organizations for the middle class, and the college-educated are very much involved with the Greek-letter fraternities.

There is no abrupt break between the middle class and the other classes. Men are more inclined to cross class lines than women and have more association with others whose class affiliations differ from their own. The middle-class person may meet upper-class people in business or school, in the course of community organization or political activities, or occasionally as neighbors. He is in contact with members of the lower class in lodges, sometimes in churches, and in labor organizations. He is likely to have a relative who has moved into the upper class and some lower-class relatives, as well, either by marriage or as a result of his own upward mobility.

The sharpest demarcation between the middle and lower status groups exists with respect to values and goals, and community participation. The middle-class husband prides himself in his stable family life, educational and financial success, home and property ownership, thrift, ambition, and high moral standards. The middle class is also eager for rights and opportunities equal to those enjoyed by whites, although as a group it seems to be slightly more conservative in regard to desegregation. Many members of the class are in positions of leadership and service in various of the more influential community organizations. While the top positions of leadership and power have not in the past been filled primarily by the middle class, its representation on this level has grown conspicuously.

The lower class differs from the middle class in most of its institutional patterns and values. The family structure is less likely to be stable. Homes broken by death or desertion are common in this group, and many of these see a succession of new "husbands" and "fathers." Employment is less certain, and temporary unemployment is common. The men are found in the dirtier manual and unskilled jobs, being employed as cutters and sweepers in the tobacco factories, janitors, night watchmen, ditch diggers, and handy men. The women work as domestics, cooks, cleaners, and unskilled factory workers. They are often members of the labor unions, but the leadership is usually recruited from the middle class.

Few have completed high school, and many do not have an elementary school education. Their children attend school, but less regularly than the middle-class children. Some finish high school and may even reach college; many drop out before they have completed their secondary education. Many lower-class Negroes in Crescent City are members of middle-class churches, but the majority of the lower class attends small fundamentalist neighborhood churches, which are splinter Baptist groups, or the many "churches" of store-front sects and cults. What little social life the lower class has is usually in connection with the church auxiliaries or the benevolent associations. Some of the men belong to lodges or veterans' groups. Members of the lower class live in the crowded, dilapidated neighborhoods of Crescent City, and their houses are sub-standard and unkempt, sometimes without indoor plumbing. It is not uncommon to have a grand-mother, cousin, aunt, or some other member of the family as part of the household unit.

The children tend to congregate around the neighbor-hood poolrooms or cafes. Some participate in organized recreational activities, an increasingly important part of lower-class neighborhood life as new facilities become available. Some may belong to the boys' clubs intended to assist lower-class children. But most of their activity is unorganized and spontaneous.

There is little awareness of community affairs among a significant proportion of the lower class. "We don't read much," and "We don't go to meetings," are frequently heard. Many members of the lower class take no daily or weekly newspaper, and even more never read a magazine. Their norms and values reflect a different world-view. Early sex knowledge, familarity with violence and illegal activities, hunger, lack of incentive or encouragement to-ward betterment—these are all part of the average lower-class Crescent City Negro's life. It would be incorrect to conclude that there is no stability in this group. The more steadily employed members are increasingly aware of mid-dle-class values and strive to conform to them. The more stable and monogamous family is becoming common. And there is some social mobility, with many members being actually in a transitional stage between the two classes. The church and the labor unions provide a focus for loyalty, and gradually lower-class Negroes are being pulled into the larger Negro community. But for many there is still apathy, family bickering, promiscuity, gambling, and little respect for the visible signs of success other than expensive automobiles and rakish clothes.

The institutional structure of Crescent City's two racial communities is rooted in the post-Civil-War period. Many of the traditional institutional forms found in the Old South were therefore never clearly defined in Crescent City Negro institutions, and organizations often borrowed their forms from white society, but through the years they have adapted themselves to the needs of a minority group. Perhaps one of the most significant features of the Crescent City Negro sub-community today is the relative stability and maturity of many of its institutions and associations, in spite of the restrictions that are still present in the biracial society of the community as a whole.

Many of the early Negro settlers in Crescent City brought with them a strong and stable patriarchal family system that served as a pattern for those who came later. There were, of course, among the early immigrants those who were former slaves and who had absorbed the values of the matriarchal structure to which slavery gave rise. Among many of the lower-class Negroes who have continued to migrate to Crescent, this influence still obtains, to a greater or lesser degree. Males are often reluctant to assume full responsibility for support of their wives and children. In turn, there are many wives who are unwilling to surrender their authority over the children and control of the family purse. Where it does exist, this pattern is gradually changing as more economic and educational opportunities become available to the lower-class population.

The Negro middle-class family tends more and more to resemble its white counterpart—a nuclear kinship unit held together by a relatively stable marriage and rarely including other relatives. It is buttressed by an ethic that opposes divorce and tends to equalize the rights and responsibilities of wife and husband. When both husband and wife have stable white-collar jobs, the family is even more likely to be equalitarian. Commonly, of course, the husband is the economic dominant.

The Negro upper-class family is also based upon a stable monogamous marriage, neolocal residence, and the economic dominance of the husband and father. But unlike the middle-class family, it is often what might be described as an expanded family system, one which takes cognizance of grandparents and a number of collateral relatives—aunts, uncles, and cousins—whether these reside in Crescent City or elsewhere. It is, in addition, a kindred. If a female member of the Alder family marries outside her class, she is still thought of as an Alder. If an Arthur marries an Alder, then the children of the marriage recognize both groups of collateral relatives. Though there may be an occasional aunt or grandparent living with the upper-class family, this is usually a device of expedience and is not a typical class pattern.

This family organization does not prevail among all upper-class Negroes, any more than it does among all upper-class whites, but it is common. It is, furthermore, a pattern of long standing that has been emulated by newcomers to the upper stratum. The long history of the stable patriarchal type of family in the upper class may help, in part, to explain the relative paucity of women who play a role in the leadership activities of the sub-community.

Aside from the family, perhaps the oldest institution in the Crescent City sub-community is the church. The first Negro church in the city, St. Paul's Episcopal, was founded in 1867. Shortly after, in 1870, the Folsom Street Methodist Church was established. Many others followed, but these were the two which attracted the early Negro leaders. With the exception of a small group at the bottom of the social scale and a small group of intellectuals at the top, the church still wields an important influence in Negro life.

From 80 to 90 per cent of the Crescent City Negroes are on the membership rolls of one of the sub-community's forty to fifty religious organizations (regular attendance is, of course, another matter). Predominantly, they are Baptists and Methodists, following the membership pattern for Negroes in general.

The Negro churches are divided along class lines, and the existence of that division is recognized by members of the sub-community as well as by many of the ministers. There are four churches which members of the upper stratum attend: St. Paul's Episcopal, Folsom Street Methodist, University Park Baptist, and First Presbyterian. The members of the "old" families and the prestige and power figures as a rule attend the first two.

Middle-class churches are almost all Baptist or Methodist. There are six recognizably middle-class churches, and among them these claim the bulk of the middle class as parishioners. Lower-class churches include innumerable small Baptist offshoots, Holiness churches, and store-front sects and cults. Often their ministers are men who have had "a calling" but who have little or no formal education. Such preachers frequently must augment their incomes by working as janitors or carpenters, or by taking similar manual-labor jobs. Small congregations and lack of funds limit the amount of effective church work that can be accomplished by most of the lower-class churches. For many members of the lower class, however, these groups provide legitimate emotional outlets, as well as avenues for recognition and fellowship. It is in his church that the lower-class person can take positions of leadership not available to him in any other areas of his life.

Though the effectiveness of the religious organizations is reduced by the very fact that the Crescent sub-community is "over-churched," the churches do have a functional relation to the needs of the sub-community that deserves emphasis.

Ministers of the leading Negro churches were, in the early years of the sub-community's growth, closely identified with the development of economic and educational institutions. The founder of St. Paul's began the first school for Negro children. Later, the Reverend Charles Stoddard, who was for many years affiliated with the Folsom Street Methodist Church, spearheaded the development of the first Negro college and was also one of the founders of a well-respected Negro financial institution. Other ministers also played key roles in the economic and educational growth of the sub-community. However, in distinction to the pattern in many areas of the United States, the minister has never been the only, or even the main, source of Negro leadership in Crescent City. The business and professional world has from the first been of equal, if not more, importance as a source of leadership.

Today the Negro religious leadership is somewhat divided in its attitude toward the place of the church in the community. There are those who feel that the church has as its primary responsibility the "uplifting" of the Negro race and who have, accordingly, concerned themselves with race relations. There are others who look upon the church as the vehicle of God to teach the true gospel. To them, its responsibility is not racial advancement but the saving of souls. As a result, some ministers are closely involved in sub-community civic, political, and race relations activities. They welcome contacts with their white colleagues and serve on interracial church committees and boards; they participate in interracial religious meetings and they speak before mixed audiences. They openly favor desegregation of all public institutions and cooperate effectively with those community leaders who are directing the fight for equality in Crescent City. This latter group is growing. Ministers who hold the opposite view, however, have remained aloof from such activities and cooperate only reluctantly, if at all, when called upon by the top Negro leadership. This disparity can be explained partly in terms of the individual minister's educational background, the class orientation of his congregation, and the philosophical and theological beliefs to which he is committed. The suggestion is also made that there are among the ministers those who are too selfish or frightened to take a forthright stand on civil rights and whose primary concern is to increase the size of their own religious organizations rather than to assist the Negro cause.

The body most influential within the religious structure is the Ministerial Council, which is made up of approximately thirty-four church representatives. There is no representation from the small sects and cults, which commonly look upon such co-operative efforts as compromises of their doctrines and suspect them of radicalism. The current president of the Ministerial Council is the pastor of one of the largest middle-class Methodist churches. He has tremendous influence over his large congregation but has taken little action as a civil rights leader. Some informants feel he is far too conservative and accommodating in his approach to desegregation and similar issues. "He won't stick his neck out" is the typical opinion of his critics. He represents the conservative wing of the Ministerial Council, though he has complied with requests to appeal to his congregation for cooperation in filing applications for reassignment of Negro children to white schools.

Until recently the most influential member of the Ministerial Council was Dr. Allen Kyser. He served as president for a number of years while pastor of St. Paul's Church. Now sixty years old, he has resided in Crescent City for twenty-eight years, serving one of the largest upper-class churches for twenty-six of those years. St.

Paul's has, according to Kyser, "1000 on the rolls, 900 who contribute financially now and then, and about 350 who come to church each Sunday."

Kyser received his Ph.D. from Yale Divinity School and for years was a liberal force in community affairs. Thought by some to have one of the finest minds in the community, he has in late years become disillusioned and discouraged about the Negro movement toward full civil rights. One of his closest friends suggests that Kyser has lost confidence in the ability of the masses of Negroes to live up to full citizenship even if the whites were willing to let them have it. Kyser is now considered to be conservative in his approach to racial issues. He feels that Negroes should "stop trying to be white" and should be proud of being Negroes. "Negroes have built up much over the years. We shouldn't let what we have slip from our hands by giving up our own institutions."

About five years ago Kyser experienced an illness which left him partially blind and contributed to his early retirement. It may also have contributed to his about face in racial matters. Most of his activities today revolve around the youth groups he organized in his early years as pastor of St. Paul's. State and national religious organizations also claim part of his time, and he teaches two days a week at the Mid-South College for Negroes.

It is hard to say exactly what his influence is today. As one economic dominant put it, "Kyser is a paradox. He is ultra-conservative on some issues and extremely liberal on others. I don't know what there is about him, but I can't leave him out as a top leader." Although most of the influential members of his congregation do not agree with his views on desegregation, he nevertheless commands wide respect. Perhaps because he was a liberal leader in the past, Kyser has not received the criticism so many of the other conservative Negro ministers have.

While the current president of the Ministerial Council represents the conservative element among the sub-community's religious leaders and Kyser is an example of a leader who has moved from the liberal to the conservative camp, the Reverend W. C. Hoover can be considered one of the most effective liberals in the religious institutions. Hoover is the minister of a small middle-class Methodist church. His congregation contains none of the influential sub-community leaders, although his church is located just beyond the University Park area. He has resided in Crescent City for twenty of his fifty-one years and at present lives across town from his church, in the East Side district. He has been active in community affairs for many years. In 1958 he became president of the local chapter of the N.A.A.C.P. His work in the N.A.A.C.P. brings him close to the Crescent Negro Council, for the local chapter does much of its work within the framework of the Council. He has been instrumental in obtaining the co-operation of other ministers in the sub-community's civil rights and political activities, and in their interest has also worked closely with many of the professional and business leaders of the sub-community. In 1958 and 1959 his wife and two children served as plaintiffs in the first Crescent City school desegregation suit.

There are other ministers in the sub-community who, like Hoover, are active in the protest movement. A few of the younger ones, such as Art Troop, are considered radical in their approach. Though their views diverge widely from those of some of the other ministers, they have been instrumental in getting the Ministerial Council to go along with the Crescent Negro Council and the N.A.A.C.P. in many protest projects that have required the co-operation of the churches.

There are three basic functions that the religious organizations perform for Crescent City Negroes today: they provide the traditional fulfillment of the spiritual needs of their membership; they serve as basic channels of communication for the sub-community leadership; and they serve as centers of organized social activity. The last two functions are of concern here because they are vitally related to the organization and structure of the sub-community.

The churches are the most comprehensive communication avenue available in the sub-community. Periodically, members of the Crescent Negro Council preside at the various churches in order to solicit support for various Council projects. In addition, the ministers themselves are called on, for instance, to encourage their parishioners to register and vote. In answer to a request of the Crescent Negro Council, the ministers were able to get over two hundred families to make formal reassignment appeals to the Crescent City school board in 1959.

As centers of social activity, the churches play an important role in the lives of many Negro citizens. The number of activities each church supports depends on its size and wealth, but most churches have some. The elaboration of church-affiliated organizations reaches rather considerable proportions in the upper- and middle-class churches especially—Girl Scout and Boy Scout troops, adults' and children's choirs, youth counseling services, credit unions, ladies' aid societies, missionary alliances, usher boards, church bands, and Hi-Y and similar youth organizations. Such "auxiliary" organizations, of course, exist in addition to the normal structured hierarchy of church organization—the boards of trustees, the ladies' altar guilds, the finance and building committees, and so forth.

Early in 1961 a Negro Muslim sect established "The Temple of Islam" in an old store on Potter Street. The fast-growing "Black Muslim" movement (with headquarters in Chicago) is militantly anti-white and anti-Christian. The local branch of this organization is unwilling to divulge the size of its membership, but rough estimates range from 15 to 200. Although it is much too early to predict what, if any, influence the Black Muslim movement will have on the religious life of the sub-community, some sub-community leaders are troubled by its presence in Crescent City.

Early residents in the Negro community were eager to educate their children. Free schools for Negroes and a few private schools appeared early in the Reconstruction period. Following Reconstruction, public education developed slowly in Crescent City, and it was only in the past two or three decades that school became a part of the normal experience for all sub-community members.

In 1950 the Negro community, under the leadership of Howard Adams, fought successfully for equal school facilities. This legal battle resulted in new school buildings, equal pay for Negro teachers, better libraries, and new textbooks. The Supreme Court decision of 1954 was for many members of the sub-community concerned with the quality of education an occasion for rejoicing. Even though much had been done to close the gap between white and Negro schools, they were still not equal. For the Negro upper and middle class, and increasingly for the lower class, education is a means of social mobility. The desegregation decision simply brought the dreams of social ascent closer to reality.

Negro teachers receive an income appreciably larger than that received by the bulk of the sub-community population. And they enjoy more prestige than do teachers in the white community. But this is not as true for Crescent City's Negro teachers as it is for Negro teachers in other parts of the country; Crescent's Negro teachers are overshadowed by the more prestigeful business and professional men and the college educators and administrators. Most of the sub-community's public school teachers fall within the middle class, though some of the wives of the younger upper-class business and professional men do teach in the city system. Generally, secondary teachers have little voice in the leadership affairs of the sub-community. Only two of the high school principals are considered to be at all active as leaders in sub-community organizations, and they are affiliated with the high school and junior high school in the upper-class area. All secondary teachers, however, are members of professional associations, and many belong to biracial community-service and welfare organizations. But few are directly involved with protest movements, politics, or desegregation.[10] This may be a reflection of what some race relations theorists have suggested as an ambivalence among Negro teachers toward desegregation. While they may favor it as an advancement toward equality for their people, they nevertheless have much to lose personally if it becomes widespread. Too, the school system has until very recently been controlled by an all-white board so that the teachers have "trod softly" for many years and find it difficult to speak out now.

Probably the two most influential associations connected with education in the sub-community are the Parent-Teachers Association Council and the Education Committee of the Crescent Negro Council. The P.T.A. Council —made up of representatives of all Negro P.T.A.'s—works actively to encourage interest and participation in school affairs among the Negro parents. It strives to raise the standards of the schools and to improve educational facilities. The group is currently headed by C. S. Driver, Manager of the Commercial Bank and Trust Company

10. This is in contrast to the findings in the New Orleans community. See Rohrer and Edmonson, *The Eighth Generation*, p. 35.

and an active member of the Crescent Negro Council. The P.T.A. works closely with the Council. It does little as a separate protest group, but has had a part in developing the strategy for securing desegregated schools. Like the Ministerial Council, it provides a channel of communication for the leaders of the Crescent Negro Council.

Basic educational plans and policies are established by the Negro Council's Education Committee. The Education Committee may request more school buses, stand in opposition to a double shift at some Negro school, petition for new facilities in an area of increasing population, propose a new school bond or consolidation of existing schools, or map new strategy to open white schools to Negro youngsters. The Committee is now chaired by Jack Simmons, a Farm and Home Insurance executive. Committee members are appointed by the C.N.C. president, Howard Adams, and the C.N.C. executive committee.

The Negro college in Crescent City was founded by the Reverend Charles Stoddard in 1907 and became a four-year liberal arts college in 1924. Reverend Stoddard served as president of the institution, Mid-South College for Negroes, for a number of years, playing a role of accommodation in order to get the necessary funds and support for the school. As a member of several boards of directors of economic organizations, he bridged the gap between the economic and educational institutions of the sub-community.

For several years Reverend Stoddard carried on an informal battle with Arnold Arthur, Jr., for recognition as spokesman for the Negro community. Some of the present "town-gown" friction may be attributed to this early rivalry between the two men, or it may be a result of a not uncommon misunderstanding between "eggheads" and "materialists." Whatever its source, today there is clearly a degree of animosity between some members of the college faculty and some businessmen. Many at the college voice resentment against the "Barton Street Boys," the businessmen. In the eyes of these professors, the businessmen seek positions of power and responsibility for their own personal profit. The businessmen, on the other hand, resent what they think is a lack of participation and initiative on the part of many of the faculty members. They are accused of being afraid to speak out because their jobs at the college are all that matter to them. As a result of this conflict, although there is co-operation between the Mid-South College and other institutional areas of sub-community life, there is not the close integration in plan and action that once there was.

The current president of Mid-South College, Dr. Albert French, is in his late fifties. Prior to taking his present post ten years ago, he served as Dean of the Graduate School in one of the better-known private Negro universities of the South. The author's first interview with Dr. French was rather strained. He had other, more pressing matters on his mind and implied that a study of Negro leaders might be rather futile. A subsequent meeting, however, was pleasant and relaxed. A scheduled forty-minute conference stretched into a two-and-one-half-hour session. He revealed a lively concern with the problems of Negro leadership, especially the role of administrators in state-supported Negro colleges. As he said, "We are caught between the wishes of our own people and those of the white state legislatures which hold the purse strings."

Although French serves on the boards of directors of the Consolidated Insurance and Realty Company and the Martin Library, most of his activities are in fulfillment of his university responsibilities and those responsibilities attendant to these—commttee memberships on biracial community-service and welfare groups. Considered a conservative by both whites and Negroes, he does not play the same role in the power structure that earlier college presidents did. Many Negroes feel that he has been much too cautious in his approach to civil rights and in his dealings with the white community and the college's biracial board of trustees. During the past three years, however, he has become more forthright in his utterances.

Some sub-community members feel Dr. Alice Bradock, chairman of the Mid-South College department of economics, has more of a public following than President French, although others disagree. Her husband, T. O. Bradock, is head of the theology department at a nearby Negro seminary. Mrs. Bradock has an aggressive and outgoing personality. She talks freely of herself and of others in the community, and she states her position on issues emphatically. Aside from her professional responsibilities, she has a heavy speaking schedule throughout the region. She is involved in politics on the national level and as a Democrat served as special consultant for the Truman Administration. She was an early Kennedy supporter. Perhaps she is better classified as a cosmopolitan than as a local leader, but she has made her position on civil rights known in both the white and Negro communities. Her husband, oddly enough, has not. He has been criticized for being "too silent." From interviews with him, I found that he was among the very few community leaders who seriously feared violence as a result of Crescent City's desegregation attempts. Time has proved his fears to be unfounded.

Another prominent member of the Mid-South College faculty is Dr. Ruth Johnson, Dean of the College of Arts and Sciences. Contrasting sharply with Mrs. Bradock, she is formal and distant to the casual observer. In the past, she has been a member of several community organizations, among them the Crescent Negro Council and the local chapter of the N.A.A.C.P., but she now takes little active part in such activities, with the exception of her efforts on behalf of the Republican Party in the city and state. She is, however, active in church and social-service organizations, and her greatest influence at present is felt in education circles through her work on a number of major local and state education committees. She has publicly stated her position in favor of desegregation of schools, though she came under criticism when she placed her niece (and ward) in a private school following the Supreme Court decision in 1954. Her colleagues, Dr. Charles Wareman of the physics department, Dr. Clarence Robb of the biology department, Dr. Jim Oldes of the history department, and Professor John Miller of the political science department are the most active faculty members in the influential Negro community organizations. All are prominent in the Negroes' fight for equality at all levels.

Such fund-raising organizations as the United Negro College Fund, the Local Scholarship Fund, and the Stoddard Memorial Fund bring leaders of various segments of the community together in united action for education. There are also several local chapters of Negro college alumni associations which cut across upper- and middle-class lines. And, of course, there are the national fraternities, which, though they are largely social, do contribute college scholarships and funds for legal and political activities in the community.

Education is beginning to assume a more important role in the stratification of the Crescent City sub-community, although its role is not yet as prominent there as it is in some Negro communities elsewhere. Negro citizens are eager that their children have the best possible educational facilities. Members of the college faculty express genuine concern because its standards do not compare with those of white colleges and universities. Students come poorly prepared, and professors—part of the vicious circle—are

often inferior to their white counterparts. Thus desegregation is seen to be important at all levels of the sub-community's educational organization. Despite the Mid-South
State legislature's maneuvers to keep desegregation at a
minimum and the unwillingness of the white community to
move toward desegregation of schools without litigation,
headway in desegregation has been made in Crescent City.

From the time Crescent City began a major economic
expansion in the latter part of the nineteenth century, the
Negro economic system has been characterized by a relative sophistication reflected by its organization into companies and corporations. We have noted how members
of the pioneering families and leaders in education, religion,
and the professions combined with early business entrepreneurs to develop the financial base of the present economic structure. Interlocking directorates guide the main
business interests, and as a result the financial organization
of the sub-community is tightly integrated.

Arnold Arthur, Sr., William Knight, and Bill Patterson,
Jr.—men whose children and grandchildren are still active
in the economic institutions—were the founders of the first
fraternal life insurance company. A few years later, Dr.
Richard Martin, Jackson Alder, Sr., and others became
affiliated with the company. In 1898 the fraternal insurance association was reorganized into the Southern Life
Insurance Company. Today the company has assets of
$61,000,000, with twenty-seven branch offices in ten states.
In 1906 the first Crescent City Negro bank was established
by the Reverend Charles Stoddard, Arnold Arthur, Jr., Bill
Patterson, and Dr. Miles Warner. Other enterprises followed. Among the more important companies today in
size and volume of business are the People's State Bank,
the Farm and Home Insurance Company, Swanson Enterprises, the Community Savings and Loan Association, the

Southland Insurance and Surety Company, and the Consolidated Insurance and Realty Company.

Early in the twentieth century, new and younger men, including some of the sons of the early economic dominants, assumed key positions in a number of firms. Some of these men had married into the pioneering families. Others, their mobility aided by their education, had made reputations for themselves in other communities. Such men as M. B. Swanson, I. N. Karns, Jack Marcy, Robert Goodman, and the sons of Martin, Conners, Arthur, Knight, Alder, and Patterson became prominent. More recently the grandchildren and great-grandchildren of the early settlers have begun to take over positions of business responsibility, accompanied by promising young businessmen brought into Crescent from elsewhere.

The transmission of wealth and economic power through inheritance and incorporation has become a tradition. Today those serving as officers and board members represent the sub-community's economic elite, its prestige elite, and in some cases its power elite. Together they compose the group defined as *economic dominants* in this study. While most board members are from Crescent City itself, membership is drawn from other urban centers of the United States as well, especially when corporations have branch offices outside Crescent. Most of the economic dominants are businessmen. The economic role of the educator, the minister, and the professional in the sub-community has gradually disappeared.

I. N. Karns, chairman of the board of Southern Life, can be considered typical of the older economic dominants still active in the sub-community. At seventy, Karns is a slight but determined and vigorous man. His business career began as an insurance and real estate salesman in Virginia. His success there led to his affiliation with South-

ern Life in a home-office post, and repeated promotions
finally led him to the presidency.

Unlike some of his older contemporaries, such as Winston Arthur, Karns did not inherit his position, although he
did later marry into the Alder family. Arthur's grandfather
was one of the founders of the first fraternal insurance
firm. His father served as president of Southern Life.
Arthur became affiliated with the organization after his
graduation from college. He worked up to the office of
vice-president and agency director, a position he retained
for nearly 30 years. Arthur and Karns came to serve as
officers and board members of most of the Negro financial
institutions in Crescent City. Prior to his retirement from
the presidency of the company in 1958, Karns was serving
on nineteen financial and service boards and commissions,
Negro and biracial, on the local, state, and national level.
Locally, aside from his economic and social-service activities, he now remains somewhat aloof from community affairs. He says he has delegated such community work
to younger members of the firm.

Karns is considered to be a moderate race leader by
his fellow citizens, and interestingly enough seems less
known among the white community leaders than many of
his business colleagues. He has given strong moral and
financial support to the civil rights battle, but claims no
active role in it. Karns has a son, two nephews, and a
brother-in-law who are affiliated with allied companies, but
outside of the economic sphere none has shown an interest
in community affairs. His son-in-law, Charles Driver, is,
however, actively associated with the most influential sub-
community associations.

When Karns retired as president to become chairman of
the board, he was succeeded to the presidency of Southern
Life by Silas Alder. Alder is a grandson of Arnold Arthur,
Jr., and a nephew of Jackson Alder, Sr., both former

presidents of Southern Life. (The youngest son of Jackson Alder is also associated with Southern Life, as well as with other companies, but he has not shown Silas' promise and is unknown outside of financial and social circles.) Silas Alder is married to a member of one of Philadelphia's upper-class Negro families. His wife has taken an active interest in his career and has gained a reputation as the leading hostess among the sub-community's elite.

Like Karns, Alder is active in the economic affairs of Crescent City and moderate in his approach to politics and social justice. One of the few Republicans among Negro leaders, he served on the Federal Housing Commission and a number of special civil rights committees under the Eisenhower Administration. He was also a United States representative to the 1957 World Health Conference. He seems popular among the white and Negro leaders, but prefers to stay out of local politics, though he does provide some financial support. In view of his leadership activities and interests, Alder, perhaps more than any other member of the community, can be considered a cosmopolitan.

Despite the presence in Crescent City of several large Negro corporations and companies, most of the sub-community's commercial enterprises are local in nature and by the broader standards of the community as a whole very small in scale. Some of these small retail, service, and manufacturing concerns have provided economic security and prestige for their owners. Cleaning establishments, cosmetic manufacturers, taxi services, garages and service stations, movie theatres, a radio station, a newspaper, and a public relations firm have prospered by catering to the segregated community. In general, however, white entrepreneurs have been able to exploit the Negro market in Crescent City far more effectively than have the Negro businessmen. The local chapter of the Negro Business League, with its auxiliary Housewives' League, has attempted to bolster Negro economic institutions through "Buy Negro" weeks and other public relations activities. Typically, the goods and services offered by the more substantial, white-operated enterprises nevertheless exert an attraction over the potential Negro customer that is far stronger than his sense of racial loyalty.

Among the more successful small businessmen is David Hale. A graduate of Howard University, Hale was born in Crescent City and lives on the edge of the University Park area in what might be considered a substantial middle-class dwelling. He began his business career in Crescent City as assistant manager of one of several concerns affiliated with Swanson Enterprises (a business that has its roots in cosmetics and undertaking, but which has expanded into many areas). Now he is co-owner of a trucking and contracting firm located in dilapidated section of the Negro business district. Despite outward appearances, Hale and his partner have a prosperous business with two small offices in other parts of Mid-South State.

Hale is firm in his conviction that Negroes must be accorded equal rights. Two years ago, with the backing of the Crescent Negro Council, he led a group of his fellow citizens in a boycott of the Crescent City Baseball Club, which was hiring Negro ball players while the city continued to practice "Jim Crow" seating in its new stadium. As a result, segregated seating in the stadium no longer obtains except as it is self-imposed.

Hale is past President of the Negro Business League. He is also an active member of the Crescent Negro Council, the N.A.A.C.P., the Masons, and the Y.M.C.A. board. The older leaders refer to him as an "up-and-coming young man." More and more frequently he seems to be appointed to serve on special policy- and decision-making committees.

Bob Healy is another well-known businessman. He is sixty years old and owns the Crescent Printing and Publish-

ing Company, which publishes the Crescent Negro newspaper. His son John has been working actively with the
newspaper since 1956, when he completed his Master's
degree at Michigan State University. The elder Healy,
who is an outspoken critic of segregation in all areas of
life, has a warm sense of humor that tends to soften his
crusading approach. A deeply religious man, he has been
a pillar of the Folsom Street Methodist Church. He is an
"old-guard" founder and member of the Crescent Negro
Council, and has worked with the Council and the
N.A.A.C.P. "when I felt I could, and alone when I felt
they were moving too slowly." It is rumored that he has
suffered financially through the years—from both the white
and Negro communities—by his reluctance to compromise
in his editorial policies on race relations. He offends many
(but fewer now than in the thirties and forties, when speaking out was rarer) and criticizes all whom he considers to
be compromising. Many in the white community do not
recognize Healy as a top Negro leader, for they consider
him too aggressive. He commands wide respect and wields
great influence, however, among the Negro rank and file
and those Negro leaders the whites do recognize. There
is some indication that his son will carry on the Healy
crusading tradition.

For the Negroes in Crescent City, manual labor, do-
mestic service, and other unskilled or semi-skilled jobs
have been the major employment. Most Negroes are still
employed in enterprises owned and operated by whites,
and the chances that the number so employed will remain
constant, and even increase, are good, for there is little
likelihood that new employment opportunities can be created within existing Negro economic institutions. The
employment of Negroes in Crescent City industry has
in recent years been affected by the advent of machinery

to perform functions previously performed by unskilled or
semi-skilled laborers. It is hoped, however, that a new
Industrial Education Center will open some new opportunities.

The most effective association working in the field of
job opportunities has been the Economic Committee of the
Crescent Negro Council. It is currently headed by David
Hale and Tom Marshall, a young attorney. This Economic
Committee has been active for many years in attempting to
broaden the job base in the sub-community. The Committee makes periodic visits to leading white employers of
the city, urging employment of qualified Negroes in non-
traditional jobs, and searches for qualified employees to fill
these positions. It works closely with the Mid-South State
Council of Human Relations, which meets periodically with
both Negro and white leaders in order to set up educational
programs aiming toward smooth incorporation of trial
Negro workers into previously closed areas. The efforts of
these groups have begun to bear fruit. Skilled Negro labor
was hired for the first time three years ago at one of the
largest industrial concerns. A few firms have begun to
hire Negro accountants and stenographers. Some companies have employed Negroes for the first time as truck
drivers. Some progress is being made in securing civil
service and other government employment.

Organization of Negro labor is restricted to the middle
and lower classes, and even there it is limited and did not
really begin to gain appreciable strength until late in 1930.
Union activity, further, is confined largely to employees of
the tobacco industry. Unions are segregated, though there
is interracial membership on joint union boards. During
the forties and early fifties some co-operation existed between the Negro and white unions, and labor seemed on
its way to being a political force in Crescent City. After
the Supreme Court decision of 1954, however, the co-

operative effort all but disappeared. Some overtures were
made by white labor leaders during the 1959 city elections,
but because white labor was among the most vocal of the
groups opposed to school desegregation, Negro labor
reacted with skepticism. Furthermore, white labor has
been unwilling to give Negro labor a more active voice in
labor affairs. It may be some time, then, before the labor
movement is a really potent force in Crescent City.

The accomplishments of organized Negro labor, on the
other hand, should not be minimized. The movement has
been instrumental in obtaining improved working conditions, fairer contract arrangements, better working hours,
higher wages, and accident, health, and retirement benefits.
But the bargaining power of Negro labor unions does not
compare with that of unions outside the South.

Like membership, labor union leadership is drawn from
the middle and lower classes. Of the Crescent City Negro
union leaders, there are three men who work actively with
the Crescent Negro Council—Stanley Lewis, Gus Harvey,
and Mac Fortune. Only one of these, however, is included
among the power nominees of the sub-community—Stanley
Lewis, who can be considered a typical labor leader. He
is a skilled worker in United Tobacco, chairman of his local
shop committee, secretary of the Negro Labor Board, and
a representative on the Crescent City Interracial Labor
Council. In addition, he is one of the officers of the
International Tobacco Workers' Union.

Labor's voice is still faint in the leadership structure of
the Negro society, but it is getting stronger. Lewis, for
instance, works within the framework of the Crescent
Negro Council, helps to deliver the labor vote, and solicits
contributions for special Negro projects. Labor has not
yet tried to buck the top Negro leadership, being handicapped, of course, by lack of its own educated and sophisticated leadership. It is becoming more articulate, though,

and probably will play a vastly more important role in the years ahead.

The Negro Labor Board serves as a cooperative body for integrating Negro efforts in the labor relations field. It draws representatives from all the tobacco locals and is effective enough to be considered one of the ten most important organizations in the Negro community. So far, it has rarely taken a stand in politics or in the general protest movement that is at variance with the policies of the Crescent Negro Council.

The medical profession has a distinctive place in the structure of the sub-community. The role played by such men as Dr. Martin and Dr. Warner in the development of Negro financial institutions during the past century has already been referred to. It was Martin who was instrumental in obtaining a hospital for the Negro population (and the first Negro library, as well). In 1898 he sought aid from Negroes and whites for the establishment of a Negro hospital and he obtained a grant for that purpose from the Lord family, early white industrialists. Later the Whitneys, who were beginning to develop financial institutions of the white community, contributed an additional sum. With these funds and contributions from the Negro community, Newell Hospital was constructed in 1901 and staffed with Negro professionals. The chief surgeon is Dr. Peter Ware, whose wife is one of the Negro social leaders. The administrative director is Martin Dart, near retirement after nearly 25 years of service. The hospital board is made up of the most prestigeful and influential Negro businessmen and professionals.

Most Negro physicians are associated with one or more of the biracial community service associations concerned with health—the Mental Hygiene Clinic, Family Service, the Health Education Council, the Cancer Fund, the Heart Fund, and others. In addition, they are members of medical professional associations—the Negro Academy of Medicine, state and national hospital associations, and medical care commissions. With but rare exceptions, however, the physicians now do not take the active part in general Negro community organizations that characterizes the careers of the "pioneer" physicians. Only one young doctor, David Baker (who is married to the daughter of Jack Marcy, one of the economic dominants), is at all active in social and political affairs. He is treasurer of the Crescent Negro Council, is active in the Boy Scouts, the Y.W.C.A., and the P.T.A., and serves on the County Democratic Committee. He does not yet rank among the top leaders of the community. This current lack of community participation by Crescent's Negro doctors conforms to the pattern elsewhere.

In medical social service, there is one young Negro social service worker who serves as director of the Health Education Division of the United Fund program. He works closely with Newell Hospital and obtains the assistance of Negroes on various United Fund committees. The Welfare Department has a Negro staff that does medical referral work, which is confined almost entirely to indigent persons. But the Negro social workers of Crescent City, unlike those of Hunter's study, are not conspicuous in the influential Negro organizations and are rarely heard from outside their own professional area.

The Negro hospital facilities are used to full capacity, but they do not take care of the medical needs of the subcommunity. The medical institutions of the white community serve the Negro population on a semi-segregated basis. Many feel the medical care at the Negro hospital to be inferior because of its lack of highly specialized professional personnel and because of the inferior medical training available to Negroes generally. Though the quality of medical service provided by Newell Hospital has improved in recent years, what is true of Negro medicine elsewhere is true of Negro medicine in Crescent City: segregation and discrimination create a vicious circle that pushes Negro standards below white.[11]   The same effect, of course, is felt in dentistry, also.   Dentists in the sub-community draw most of their patients from the upper and middle classes, and those few dentists who are in practice seem to fare well financially.   Dr. John Barron is one of the older and more successful Negro dentists.   He owns an attractive office in the better section of the main Negro business district.   He has served on a number of administrative boards and service organizations in the sub-community, and is at present a member of the biracial board of trustees of Mid-South College.   Others in the dental profession are rarely involved in sub-community civic and political affairs.

In sharp contrast to the role of the medical profession is that of the legal profession.   The latter group is actively engaged in a wide variety of community affairs—especially in political and protest efforts.   The legal structure began to evolve in the sub-community in the 1920's.   By 1930 there were four practicing Negro attorneys—three with small private practices and one serving as a corporation attorney.   Two of these men are still in practice: Harry Erickson, who is the lawyer for several of the Negro financial institutions, and Hugh Grant, who is soon to retire from private practice.

That Crescent City attracted Negro lawyers as early as it did is significant, for the number of Negroes in law in the twenties and thirties was very small.   In 1930 some southern states, among them Alabama and Mississippi had no

11. For a recent analysis of the Negro medical profession, see Dietrich C. Reitzes, *Negroes and Medicine* (Cambridge, Mass.: Harvard University Press, 1958).

more than four or five Negro attorneys-at-law within their borders. Like other professionals, lawyers have suffered from a lack of adequate educational opportunities. During the past two decades, however, in state after state they have had white law schools opened to them. These expanding educational possibilities have combined with more equitable treatment of Negro litigants in most of the courts throughout the country to make law a dignified and lucrative profession for Negroes. Too, the rise in the number and complexity of suits for Negro rights has opened up the area of constitutional law for Negro lawyers. Of course, in Crescent City the presence of a Negro upper and middle class has provided the legal profession with a desirable clientele whose legal problems usually are commercial. More and more of the Negro masses, however, are turning to the lawyers of the sub-community for assistance in civil and criminal actions and for private legal advice.

Mid-South College has a law school that was in 1948 one of the six Negro law schools in the United States. Several of the lawyers in Crescent City obtained at least part of their training there. Recently the school of law at the originally white University of Mid-South State has also been desegregated, so that a few Negro law students in the area have access to its superior facilities. In addition to the faculty at the Mid-South College Law School, there are at present fifteen men in the sub-community who act as legal advisors. Thirteen are practicing attorneys. Of the other two, Jackson Alder, Jr., works full time as legal advisor for the Southern Life Insurance Company, and Howard Adams, president of one of the Negro financial enterprises, serves on the legal staff of the local chapter of the N.A.A.C.P.

Many of the Negro lawyers in private practice are also on the legal advisory staff of the N.A.A.C.P. and have been instrumental in preparing suits against Crescent City in various civil rights areas.   Harris Erickson, O. G. Sherwood, Tom Marshall, and Charles May occupy key positions in the Crescent Negro Council and work closely with other sub-community leaders.   Erickson is the wealthiest of the group.   As one of the early attorneys, he trod very carefully in order to avoid offending the white legal forces. It is only in the past ten years that he has become active in civil rights cases, though he, like the others, is also receiving criminal and civil cases.   Erickson and the other prominent attorneys of the Crescent sub-community often serve as counsel for Negro defendants in other parts of the Mid-South State because of their growing reputations as able and effective trial lawyers.

Sherwood has been in practice in the sub-community for approximately twenty-two years and is most outspoken in his approach to problems facing the Negro in the South. Like Bob Healy of the Crescent Printing and Publishing Company, he is an old hand at protest.   Before moving his practice to Crescent City, Sherwood practiced law in a nearby state, where in 1935 he initiated one of the earliest lawsuits in the South against a segregated state university. The case was lost, though, as Sherwood says, "not for long." As an attorney in Crescent City, he has continued the fight as legal counsel for both the local and state N.A.A.C.P.

Marshall, who is another legal crusader for Negro rights, is relatively new in Crescent City.   A serious and aggressive young attorney of 35, he is not new to the legal struggle for desegregation in public education.   Marshall respresents the militant wing of the young leadership in the city and is willing—indeed eager—to be in the forefront of the struggle.   He was born in Mid-South State, but has lived in Crescent City for only seven years.   He attended Atlanta University, then came to Mid-South College to attend law school.   During the late 1940's, he was one of the successful plaintiffs in the court action against segregation in the law school of the University of Mid-South State. He has since joined a small law firm and works closely with Sherwood on much of the civil rights litigation throughout the state. One of his first successful cases in Crescent City involved the daughter of Charles Driver, who was plaintiff in a suit to open the state university to Negro undergraduates. Marshall is active in many of the Negro and biracial community associations—the United Fund, The Negro Business League, the Boy Scouts, the American Legion, and the Crescent Negro Council.

Political participation among the Negro citizens of Mid-South state is now fairly widespread. A state "grandfather clause" was declared unconstitutional by the United States Supreme Court in 1915, and a poll-tax requirement was eliminated in 1920. Negroes in Crescent City began to get their foothold in politics following the organization of the Crescent Negro Council in the 1930's. Political activity has increased, as has voting registration and participation at the polls. Negroes have for some years been represented in the Crescent County Democratic and Republican organizations, although participation in the latter party has had little effect within the community. Those few leaders whose allegiance is to the Republican Party usually work only on the national level, as the party has little power at the local and state levels. Their role in the national party is largely the result of what might be described as "racial appointments" made to give token representation to minorities with potential political power. One leader, T. O. Bradock, does work on the local level and was recently elected vice-chairman of the Republican county committee.

The political strength of the sub-community lies with the Democratic Party organization. Negro leaders feel that this is where it must remain, at least for the present, if they are to have access to bargaining power. But as V. O. Key has pointed out, the politics of the "one-party" South is actually a politics of faction.[12]   This is true in Mid-South State at the local, county, and state levels.   Conservative and moderate-liberal wings of the party vie for control of party committees.   Though city politics is supposedly non-partisan, there too the anti-Negro and anti-labor factions of the conservative wing exist, and the party has often taken the views of these two factions into account, as well as those of the more moderate businessmen and professionals.   It is with this latter faction that the bulk of the Negro community has allied itself politically.

In 1953 political organization was effective enough in the minority community to elect the first Negro to city office.   As in many urban centers of the South, Negroes in Crescent City now hold the balance of power because of their block voting, a situation that irritates and frustrates many of the whites.   The white newspapers usually make much of united Negro political activity in their reports on community elections and often suggest that certain issues are doomed by virtue of Negro opposition even before votes have actually been cast.   One has only to scrutinize the tabulations of voting by precincts to see that bloc voting has been, in reality, quite effective.   For example, in the 1957 elections the moderate candidate for mayor, incumbent Murphy, received 621 out of 658 votes in the largest Negro precinct and 549 out of 573 votes in the second largest Negro precinct.

It is, in many respects, difficult to define a political structure in the sub-community that is distinct from other socially significant institutions and associations.   By far the most powerful political group is the Crescent Negro

12. V. O. Key, *Southern Politics in State and Nation* (New York: Alfred A. Knopf, 1950), p. 16.

Council, with its Political Action Committee. Political scientists have tended to define such Negro organizations in purely political terms—but to do so is to simplify, reduce, and obscure their broader social significance. As we have observed, the Council operates effectively in many institutional areas of Negro social organization. *One* of its major functions is political action, and its endeavors in this area have been increasingly successful. The local chapter of the N.A.A.C.P. also has a political orientation, but its membership overlaps that of the Crescent Negro Council (i.e., the chairman of the Legal Redress Committee of N.A.A.C.P. is the chairman of the Political Action Committee, O. G. Sherwood) and its leaders work within the Council framework. The Council's Political Action Committee solicits aid from a wide variety of groups in its political program. I have mentioned the role of the churches, fraternal groups, and labor unions, which are channels through which the masses of the sub-community can be reached. Decisions about which candidates to back, which issues to favor or oppose, and which Negroes to run for office, are made by the Council Executive Committee in conjunction with the Political Action Committee. Policies made and decisions reached are presented before the total Council membership (which includes representatives of all Negro associations and organizations, plus all interested citizens). Once the Council as a whole has given its formal approval, precinct committeemen, representatives of other organizations, and Council leaders communicate that approval to the sub-community as a whole. Negro voters are "assisted" in making their choices by the type of flyer shown in Fig. 2. In contrast to the "assistance" given in the days when Jackson Alder, Sr., and Dr. Stoddard held control, the citizens of the sub-community are no longer told for whom they *must* vote.

The Political Action Committee of the Crescent Negro Council
Recommends the Following Candidates:

For Sheriff
    Gary M. Marshall

For County Commissioners
    Arnold Craig
    Philip F. Patrick
    David S. Stanton
    Harold L. Longmire

For Constable: Crescent Township
    Lloyd S. Roberts

For County Board of Education
    Robert Cranston
    John L. Doyle
    Peter N. Walters

For State House of Representatives
    Harold N. Stratton
    Jack Cort, Jr.

For State Senator
    Douglas O. Potter

Campaign Headquarters—Crescent Publishing Company Offices—
136 Potter St.

FIG. 2.   Election flyer distributed by C.N.C. throughout Negro community.

Final political policies are established by the sub-community only after frank maneuvering and trading have obtained the maximum of benefits which the white leadership is willing to provide in return for Negro political support. In the sub-community there are no political bosses, ward heelers, and professional or career politicians, in the true senses of the words. Those who are political leaders are almost invariably leaders in other segments of the sub-community's institutional structure. To discuss individual Crescent City Negroes as "political leaders" is, then, somewhat misleading. It is usually by virtue of their prestige and power positions in other areas that they are able to obtain power in the political area, not vice versa. Of course, this relation does not always obtain in other communities, either Negro or white, but in Crescent City political structure seems clearly to derive from other sectors of institutional life.

Let us take, for example, the case of Howard T. Adams, president of the Farm and Home Insurance Corporation.

Adams' name is mentioned whenever persons of power and leadership are discussed. He is forty-nine years old and has resided in Crescent City for twenty-eight years. Coming from South Carolina after finishing his college education, he began his business career as an agency officer for one of the bonding and real estate companies. Soon he transferred to the Farm and Home Insurance firm. His wife is the daughter of M. H. Martin, of the sub-community's upper-class. Adams' son is a junior at Harvard, and he hopes to send his daughter to Oberlin.

Adams is a very reserved, soft-spoken, dignified individual whose appearance commands respect. Considered a liberal by his peers, he is a polished and effective spokesman of his people. He is admired by most Negro community members for his unselfish efforts to secure equal opportunities for Negroes in Crescent City and elsewhere. While there are a few dissenters who feel he seeks and thrives on power, he is the community member most frequently mentioned as having the interests of the Negro community at heart. He expresses his attitude toward desegregation as, "Set your policies and plans carefully; move firmly forward."

As a member of the financial world Adams holds positions as officer or board member of most of the major Negro firms in Crescent. His community activities are wide. He serves on the board of trustees of nearly all of the major Crescent City Negro (and many white) organizations and associations—the hospital, the library, the boys club, the park foundation, the scholarship fund, the United Fund, the 4-H, Urban Renewal, the Democratic Executive Committee, the Crescent Committee for Industrial and Economic Expansion, and many others. Adams' activities, like those of Karns, are not confined to the local scene, for he also serves on several state and national policy-making boards or commissions. In 1958,

Adams served as United States representative to a United Nations commission in Pakistan. He has long been a pillar of the Crescent Negro Council, holding positions of highest importance. He recently became president of the Council, but his place in the organization and structure did not shift; it simply became more explicit.

Very often Howard Adams is linked with Steven Mc-Donald. More often than not, their names appear in one-two order on leader-selection lists. McDonald, in contrast to Adams, is an expansive, talkative person. He is very much aware of his position as a leader and quite proud of the role he plays. At 48 he is executive vice-president of the People's State Bank and serves on the board of the Farm and Home Insurance Company, the Community Savings and Loan Association, the Consolidated Insurance and Realty Company, and Swanson Enterprises. McDonald's mother was related to the Arthur family and he himself is married to a Patterson. Of all the top leaders, his home is perhaps the most pretentious. In the heart of the University Park section, it is a two-story brick colonial, set well off the avenue.

Like Adams, McDonald is interested in the political progress of the sub-community and is a member of the Mid-South Democratic Executive Committee and the Crescent Negro Council. He was elected to the Crescent City Council in 1957, to become the second Negro to serve in a city office. McDonald is also regarded as a liberal by most of his fellow workers. Some believe McDonald is often Adams' puppet. Certainly the two men work closely together in all activities and have a firm grasp on the political affairs of the minority community.

Nathan Banks preceded McDonald on the City Council. As general manager of the Community Savings and Loan Association, Banks is another of the active economic dominants. He serves, as well, on the boards of several

other firms.   Now in his middle fifties, he is a tall, friendly
man with a twinkle in his eye.   His ancestors settled in
Maryland as freedmen about the end of the eighteenth
century, and he prizes a picture of the attractive white clapboard cottage that was his family's homestead.   As he
says, "I married no one of importance in this community,
but just worked my way up from my own beginnings."
Banks has one child, a daughter, to whom he is very close.
She is married to a young insurance salesman who is pres-
ently with the Baltimore branch office of Southern Life.
While Banks would like very much to have the pair return
to Crescent City, he said in one interview that perhaps it
would be better for his young grandson "Nat" if they remained in an area which could afford him more favorable
opportunities.

Banks considers himself a moderate and in the days
following the 1954 Supreme Court decision made public
statements to the press calling for temperateness on all sides
in upholding the decision.   "Time is needed," said Banks.
"We must be patient a little longer and move slowly—but
we must move."   The first Negro to be elected to a political
position in Crescent City, he was a successful candidate in
1953.   He was opposed by the white community at the
time, but subsequently won the support of many white
leaders and had been assured of their backing if he decided to seek re-election in 1957.   Following his decision
not to run again, the City Council appointed him to the
school board—another first.   As a result of friendships
begun when they were City Council members, Banks has
very close, though covert, relationships to two of the top
white power leaders.

Occasionally a pressure group will emerge from the
Negro community and seek a hearing before the City
Council or some other administrative organization.   Pres-
sure groups commonly work through the Crescent Negro

Council, from which they receive a hearing and often offers of assistance in realizing their desires. Occasionally white political and civic leaders approach a Negro group like the P.T.A. or the Ministerial Council to solicit support for some project. But with rare exceptions the Negro organizations concerned consult the appropriate Crescent Negro Council committees before replying to such overtures. The Political Action Committee of the Council and the local chapter of the N.A.A.C.P. can be regarded as true pressure groups. They withhold support from issues or candidates until they obtain concessions "in writing—promises are too easily forgotten." The future looks bright for the political process in the sub-community. Mid-South State's traditionally moderate approach to Negro voting rights and the organizational stability of the Negro community have created a more favorable political picture than exists in many other parts of the South.

During the course of my study, Negro leaders and community members were asked to name the important or influential organizations within the Negro community. Many of the organizations they identified have been treated already in terms of the institutional structures with which they are associated. The list includes the Crescent Negro Council, the local chapter of the N.A.A.C.P., the Negro Business League, the Ministerial Council, the Negro Labor Board, the P.T.A. Council, the Y.W.C.A., and the Masons. Some of these are protest organizations and some are political, racial-uplift, recreational or community service, or economic organizations. The Crescent Negro Council cuts across these many sectors of community activity. In some ways it can be regarded as the coordinating body for all the Negro community organizations, guiding their activities and interests in the direction of a united Negro protest and improvement effort. The Council is composed of five standing committees: Civic, Economic, Educational, Legal Redress, and Political Action. The chairmen and members of these standing committees are drawn from the leadership of many of the other important Negro organizations. The executive committee works closely with each standing and special committee, with a few men dominating the policy- and decision-making. Perhaps one of the primary reasons for the sub-community's extraordinary success in its endeavors to gain rights and privileges for its people is the effective co-ordination that the Crescent Negro Council makes possible.

There are, of course, many organizations in Negro Crescent City besides the most influential ones discussed here, which represent only the most vocal or powerful opinion in the sub-community. A number of fraternal associations and lodges, for example, contribute to the social life of their members, who are commonly drawn from the middle and lower classes. In addition, many such organizations have passed resolutions opposing segregation and discrimination, and many of them contribute funds to support civil rights activities. Their economic, social, and political power has, however, long since disappeared in Crescent City.

The few Negro recreational and service agencies working with the youth of the sub-community are strongly supported by the leading citizens. The Scouts, the Y.W.C.A., the Y.M.C.A., the Avon Boys Club, the Park Hill Recreation Center, the Agnes Swanson Nursery, and the many neighborhood recreation centers have programs which strive to reach children of all classes. They are most effective among youth of the middle and, in some cases, of the lower classes. The Y.W.C.A. has sponsored social groups in the various schools and among young adults, and programs for housewives and working women, as well. It also maintains a dormitory for young working girls which has contributed to the integration of its occupants into the larger community. The boards and committees of the recreational and service organizations in Crescent City draw their members from among the power and prestige leaders. At these higher levels, there is co-operation with the corresponding organizations in the white community. Joint board, committee, and staff meetings and luncheons are common. Occasionally joint programing has been attempted.

There are a number of neighborhood betterment organizations which have done a significant job. Of these the Dayton Council is the best known, but groups such as the West Side Betterment League, the Brown Council, and the Lennox Park Betterment Committee have also been successful. They instill neighborhood spirit, develop recreation facilities, encourage pride in neat homes and lawns, and obtain better streets and street lighting.

In organizations that are still rooted in the local white community, Negro participation is gradually being accepted. There is participation, of course, in biracial associations on the state and national levels, and it, too, is increasing. In addition, within the Negro organizations themselves there is a growing co-ordination in policy and action. The significance of the geographic extension of Negro leadership outside the sub-community, while not yet great, is nevertheless appreciable. For the masses of Negroes, this broader organizational life may as yet have little apparent effect, but to the extent that it gives added experience to Negro leaders and increases their prestige and influence in the eyes of the white community, it does contribute to the sub-community as a whole.

It was my contention at the beginning of this chapter that the leadership and power of the sub-community could not be effectively understood without some insight into the social organization and structure found there. It is a basic assumption that society is so structured that power and prestige are unevenly distributed among its members. Among the most important indicators of the status and power of groups or individuals is their place in the stratification systems and within the major institutional organizations. All such relationships are reciprocal, as we have seen, and it is precisely this interdependence that establishes the dynamism of the community under consideration.

CHAPTER IV

IDENTIFYING CRESCENT CITY'S NEGRO LEADERSHIP

L IKE BARTH[1] and Hunter,[2] I found an identifiable structure of leadership in the Negro sub-community of Crescent Ctiy. In contrast to Barth's conclusions, however, my own evidence indicated that many of the Negro leaders are power wielders, for they hold positions of importance in the total community, as well as in the sub-community.

I began my investigation of Negro leaders in Crescent City by applying three variations of the power attribution method for identifying leaders, with three groups as informants—Negro leaders themselves, white leaders, and a general sub-community sample. How much white leaders knew about the minority power structure I was not aware. Some scholars have believed that the minority community is better acquainted with the characteristics of the white community than whites are with the characteristics of the Negro community. Hunter and others have found little consciousness among either Negroes or whites of the identities of the real leaders in the two racial groups. I hypothesized that the same would be true in Crescent City also, but the data did not bear this hypothesis out.

1. Ernest A. T. Barth and Baha Abu-Laban, "Power Structure and the Negro Sub-Community," *American Sociological Review,* 24 (February, 1959), pp. 75-76.
2. Floyd Hunter, *Community Power Structure* (Chapel Hill: University of North Carolina Press, 1953), pp. 114-50.

I further was not sure what to expect from the sub-community sample, for it was possible that, as has been suggested elsewhere, the "articulate followers" set the pace, so to speak, for leaders in the Negro community. My investigation could reasonably enough have shown that those high on the socio-economic scale were highly perceptive of the power leaders, while those lower on the scale had little or no knowledge of the leaders. Since, however, I was already acquainted with the institutional and organizational structure of the Negro community, I suspected I might find significant similarities among the identifications made by Negro leaders and by the sub-community as a whole. This, in fact, proved to be the case.

I defined the *leader* as an individual whose behavior affects the patterning of behavior within the community at a given time. A total of 189 Negroes were nominated as leaders by the three groups of informants. Of these, 54 received one or more nominations as key decision-makers. The greatest proportion of votes from each of the three nominating groups was obtained by 31 leaders, and it is with a majority of these 31 that the study is largely concerned. Some leaders have already been introduced to the reader, and others will be introduced in the pages to come.

As data to be presented later will document, all individuals playing a leading role in various community issues were identified as power nominees, but not all of the power nominees played a decision-making role in the issues selected for discussion. I use the term *power nominee* to refer to the 31 leaders who were identified as the most powerful or influential by the three groups of informants. The group of power nominees can be subdivided into *top power* and *sub-power* nominees according to sociometric ratings. The term *lesser leader* is used to refer to those individuals who were not identified as power nominees or observed to be power leaders. The term *power leader* identifies those individuals who in practice played the most active roles in community issues.

A chain referral or "snowball" technique was utilized in the Negro leadership poll. The design was, in brief: (1) men of "experience" or "experts" in the field of study[3] were consulted for assistance in the identification of key individuals in the community; (2) the key individuals named by the "experts" became the key informants and were in turn interviewed for assistance in identifying the influential leaders in all aspects of community life; (3) the identifications made by the key informants were employed as a basic list of persons to be interviewed in the effort to determine who the reputed power leaders were; (4) additional nominations made by persons on this basic list were added to what became the master interviewing list; (5) those individuals who by sociometric selection were reputed to be most powerful were then interviewed with regard to their attitudes, roles, and actions on basic issues and their interaction with others in the community in connection with such issues.

A total of 110 selections were obtained by the snowball technique. Of these, 54 individuals received more than 2 nominations. These composed the master list for

3. The use of the term "expert" here is not to be confused with its common use in power studies in which the "panel of experts" selects names from a compiled list. The term "expert" as employed in the present project is taken, rather, from Jahoda, Deutsch, and Cook, where it has reference to a special role: "The information from . . . the area to be studied almost invariably must be supplemented by a number of unstructured interviews with people who have had considerable experience in the field to be investigated. In addition to obtaining recommendations about potential informants, these preliminary interviews have the purpose of sketching the dimensions of the issues . . . to be covered. . . . Marie Jahoda, Morton Deutsch, and Stuart W. Cook, *Research Methods and Social Relations* (New York: The Dryden Press, 1951), pp. 38-39. For a more complete description of the method used at this and other stages of the study, see Appendix B.

interviewing purposes. The 54 leaders listed include 4 women and 50 men, ranging in age from twenty-eight to eighty-one. Their mean age is 51.1 years. Slightly more than 41 per cent were born in Mid-South State, and all but two of the remaining leaders were born in other southern states. The mean length of residence in Crescent City is 24.7 years. All but four of the 54 leaders had some college education, and 38 received graduate training. The professions claim 27 of this basic list of leaders; banking, finance, and insurance engage 11; small business and commerce are represented by 10 persons; government and community service have 3 representatives, as does labor. Seventy-four per cent of the leaders are dependent upon salaries for sustenance, although several of these have fairly extensive savings and investments.

TABLE 1

NEGRO LEADERS RANKED ACCORDING TO NUMBER OF VOTES RECEIVED FROM OTHER NEGRO LEADERS IN LEADERSHIP POLL

Leaders	Number of Nominations	Number of Mutual Choices
Howard Adams	44	6
Steven McDonald	39	5
I. N. Karns	27	2
Nathan Banks	26	4
Silas Alder, R. Healy	18	3,4
Albert French	12	2
William C. Hoover	9	0
Howard I. Erickson	8	1
David Hale, Allan Kyser,	7	1,1
O. G. Sherwood		2
Charles Wareman, Y. O. Bradock	6	2,1
John Miller	5	0
Alice Bradock	4	1
M. B. Swanson, D. E. Jackson	3	1,0
E. S. Smith, R. E. Laroux,	2	1,0
Ruth Johnson, C. E. Driver		0,0
Tom Marshall, Jack Simons,	1	0,0
Stanley Lewis, Conrad May,		1,0
S. T. Parsons, Miles Conners		0,1

TABLE 2
REASONS GIVEN FOR SELECTION OF POWER NOMINEES BY OTHER LEADERS IN NEGRO LEADER POLL

Leader	REASONS				
	Position			Personal Attributes	Organizational Activity and Civic Service
	Occupational	Political	Civic		
Adams	18	—	8	21	12
McDonald	7	11	12	5	6
Karns	19	—	4	10	5
Banks	4	8	3	10	4
Alder	6	3	5	5	5
Healy	6	—	—	16	5
French	14	—	—	4	2
Hoover	—	—	3	2	6
Erickson	7	1	—	3	1
Hale	2	—	4	5	5
Kyser	4	—	—	2	3
Sherwood	—	2	—	2	2
Wareman	—	1	5	3	3
T. Bradock	1	—	1	—	8
Miller	2	—	1	1	3
A. Bradock	1	—	—	1	3
Swanson	3	—	—	—	—
Jackson	1	—	—	4	1
Smith	1	—	—	2	2
Laroux	1	—	—	—	—
Johnson	1	2	—	—	—
Driver	—	—	—	—	2
Marshall	—	—	—	—	3
Simmons	—	—	1	—	1
Lewis	1	—	—	—	—
May	1	—	—	—	—
Parsons	1	—	—	—	1
Conners	2	—	—	—	—

Informants were asked to nominate at least five persons whom they regarded as most influential in the Negro community. In Table 1 leaders are ranked by the total number of nominations they received and by the number of nominations they received from others included in the table ("mutual choices"). It should be noted that only 28 of the 54 leaders on the chain-referral master list received one or more votes as power nominees. Of these, 12 received 8 or more votes and 7 received 12 or more nominations. Of the top 12, 6 represent the major Negro financial and banking firms; 2 are attorneys; 2 are ministers; 2 are self-employed; 1 is a college administrator. Of the top 7 nominees, all but 2 represent principal financial firms of the minority community.

Of special interest are the reasons given by the respondent leaders for their choices. These vote justifications are classified in Table 2. Some respondents gave only one reason; others gave two, indicating that they felt both to be of equal importance. With few exceptions, the reasons fell into three categories: institutional position; personal attributes; and civic service in the community. The first category, institutional position, includes family status, business and professional positions, political office, and civic or associational positions. The second, personal attributes, includes courage, special training or experience, poise, individual status, intelligence, honesty, morality, respectability, dignity, and reliability. The third, organizational activity, includes performance, reliability, activity, number of organizational memberships, degree of service, and success in fulfillment of responsibility.

In most instances, then, choices are related to the bases of power[4] that can be used to influence others in order to obtain more power, though they do not constitute power in and of themselves—such bases as position, status, wealth, courage, knowledge, and activity. Accordingly, the twenty-eight leaders are, most strictly, not people known to be powerful, but people known to have access to sources of power.

There were two reasons for sampling the Negro community. First, the responses of the community sample

4. See, for example, Robert Bierstedt, "An Analysis of Social Power," *American Sociological Review,* 15 (December, 1950), pp. 730-38; and Harold D. Lasswell and Abraham Kaplan, *Power and Society* (New Haven: Yale University Press, 1950), pp. 97-99.

were seen as a possible check on the reliability of the Negro leadership poll data. Second, I was interested in learning how effective patterns of communication and interaction were between leaders and their followers. Did the people in general know who the leaders were and what they were doing? Did they see community problems—especially desegregation—in the same light as their leaders saw them? Suchman, Williams, and others have postulated that Negro leaders, in general, are not powerful initiators of action among their followers, but rather are individuals who are functionally related to and implicated in a system of mutual obligations and expectations with the followers, established and maintained in group interaction.[5] Moreover, the Cornell memorandum on desegregation has posited that the further the minority community leader strays from the ideas and sentiments of the "motivated and articulate followers" in the community, the greater is the chance that he will prove unsuccessful as a leader. Who are the "motivated and articulate followers," if there are such, and how closely do the power leaders lead, follow, or interact with this group? These questions suggested other problems, such as the necessity of differentiation between community respondents on the basis of social class—the assumption being that the lower the social class, the less "articulation and motivation" would be found.

Thus, rather than using a random sample, I decided to use a *stratified areal sample* based initially on sub-community residential areas. Because I was concerned with class differentials and because a majority of the Negro residential blocks in Crescent City could be presumed to be lower class, it was necessary to make some arbitrary distinction among residential areas on the basis of the class

5. Edward A. Suchman *et al.*, *Desegregation: Some Propositions and Research Suggestions* (New York: Anti-Defamation League of B'nai B'rith, 1958), p. 69.

of housing in them.   Negro residential districts were mapped into upper-, middle-, and lower-class areas by a variety of techniques.   Individual blocks were classed by combining scores of the majority of the dwelling units in the block with the score of the dwelling area as a whole. Blocks were drawn from each "residential class area," numbered, and block numbers for sampling selected from a table of random numbers.   Field workers, upon visiting a specific house, would make a second appraisal of housing type which served as *one* criterion for determining the individual informant's position in the social-class scale.[6]

In order to satisfy my desire for a check on the findings obtained from the Negro leadership poll, in a series of questions Negro citizens were asked to identify basic community problems and then to associate leaders with issues. Second, the citizen-respondents were asked to list the five most powerful Negro leaders.   The replies were calculated to uncover leaders who were perceived to play specialized roles in community life, as opposed to those who operated in more general areas of community activity.

Arbitrarily, the size of the community sample was set at 300, or 100 interviews from each class.   Actually, a total of 283 completed interviews were held—98 lower class, 100 middle class, and 85 upper class.   Table 3 provides a statistical picture of the personal-social characteristics of the sample informants, by class.

Some 25 per cent of the respondents were male. Twelve per cent of the interviewees were 24 years of age or less; 42.8 per cent were 25 to 44 years old; 35.3 per cent were 45 to 64 years old; and 9.8 per cent were 65 years old or older.   With regard to the respondents' marital status, 14.2 per cent were single; 13.3 per cent were widowed; 67.6 per cent were married; and 5 per cent were separated or divorced.   Of those interviewed, nearly 30 per cent had

6. See Appendix B for a detailed account of method used.

TABLE 3
PERSONAL-SOCIAL CHARACTERISTICS OF SUB-COMMUNITY RESPONDENTS, BY CLASS PERCENTAGE

Characteristics	Upper Class	Middle Class	Lower Class
Sex:			
Male	27.1	22.0	24.5
Female	72.9	78.0	75.5
Marital Status:			
Single	8.2	12.0	22.5
Married	77.5	75.0	51.0
Widowed	10.6	11.0	17.3
Separated-Divorced	3.6	2.0	9.2
Number of Children:			
1-3	63.6	55.0	39.8
4-6	5.9	11.0	21.5
7-over	1.2	3.0	9.2
none	29.3	31.0	29.5
Years Residence in Crescent City:			
1-10	24.7	12.0	13.2
11-20	27.0	22.0	23.5
21-over	48.3	66.0	63.3
Reside in Holis District:	100.0	77.0	54.1
Type of Housing:			
Upper	77.8	17.0	—
Middle	22.2	76.0	23.4
Lower	—	7.0	76.6
Rent	5.9	34.0	88.9
Own	94.1	66.0	11.1
Occupation: (Head of House)			
Professional	59.0	9.0	—
Business and White Collar	32.0	15.0	5.1
Services and Skilled Labor	9.0	56.0	20.0
Semi- and Unskilled	—	20.0	74.9
Education:			
None	—	2.0	7.2
Grade School	1.2	26.0	49.0
High School	9.5	45.0	42.8
College/Graduate School	85.9	23.0	—
Technical	3.4	4.0	1.0
Church Affiliation:			
Upper	67.1	34.0	3.1
Middle	14.1	35.0	19.4
Lower	2.4	24.0	66.3
Other Religious Organization or None	16.4	7.0	11.2

no children; 52.4 per cent had three or fewer children; 13 per cent had 4 to 6 children; and 4.9 per cent had 7 or more children.

Upper-class heads of households were, as would be expected, concentrated in professional, business, and other white-collar occupations, with 91 per cent falling in these categories. Sixty-one per cent of the middle class were found in service, skilled-labor, and small-business occupations. Approximately 94 per cent of the lower class were clustered in service and semi- and unskilled jobs. In addition to information about occupations, data were solicited on employment status. It was found that 80.5 per cent of the males and 42.2 per cent of the females were gainfully employed. Nearly 3 per cent of the males were unemployed; 2.3 per cent worked part time; 2.3 per cent were temporarily laid off; 7.9 per cent were retired; 1.4 per cent were unable to work; and 2.8 per cent were not in the labor force. Seven and one-half per cent of the females were unemployed; 9.3 per cent were working part time; and 28 per cent, not in the labor force, were full-time housewives.

The educational background of the sub-community respondents is also revealing. Of the total sample, 3.2 per cent had had no schooling, 26.4 per cent had obtained some elementary education, 33.6 per cent had acquired some secondary education, 34.1 per cent had received some college training, and 2.8 per cent had attended technical or vocational training schools. Only 6.4 per cent of the sample indicated that they had no church affiliation.

In general, the community members had been residents of Crescent City for some length of time. Some 59.7 per cent of the interviewees had resided in the community from 21 to 40 years, and only 16.3 per cent had been in the city for less than ten years. Born in Mid-South State were 79.2 per cent; 2.1 per cent were born in other than southern states. Thus, the sample represents a fairly homogeneous group from the standpoint of regional and community background.

TABLE 4
NEGRO LEADERS RANKED ACCORDING TO NUMBER OF VOTES RECEIVED AS "ISSUE LEADERS" IN SUB-COMMUNITY SAMPLE POLL

Leader	I	II	III	IV	V	VI	VII	VIII	IX	X	XI	Total Vote	%**
McDonald	23	20	6	3	3	6	6	3	6	—	1	77	18.4
Adams	8	16	8	2	4	5	10	2	7	3	—	65	15.6
Banks	7	9	7	2	5	2	5	—	1	—	—	38	9.1
Karns	4	10	1	3	1	1	2	—	1	—	—	23	5.5
Healy	1	6	1	1	—	2	2	1	3	1	—	18	4.3
Jackson	3	5	1	—	1	2	2	—	1	—	1	16	3.8
Hopkins	—	—	—	14	—	—	—	—	—	—	—	14	3.3
Erickson	—	4	—	—	6	—	1	1	1	—	—	13	3.1
Alder	3	2	—	1	1	1	2	—	1	—	—	11	2.6
T. Downs	4	—	—	4	—	—	2	—	—	—	1	11	—
Wareman	—	2	—	1	1	1	2	2	—	—	—	9	2.2
Sherwood	—	2	1	—	2	2	—	1	—	—	—	8	1.9
Swanson	5	1	—	1	—	—	—	—	—	1	—	8	—
Marshall	—	3	2	1	2	—	—	—	—	—	—	8	—
Carver	—	3	4	—	—	—	—	—	—	—	—	7	1.7
Miller	—	—	3	—	1	2	—	1	—	—	—	7	—
R. Johnson	—	2	—	—	—	4	—	—	—	—	—	6	1.4
French	—	—	3	—	—	3	—	—	—	—	—	6	—
Robbins	—	2	—	2	—	—	1	1	—	—	—	6	—
Smith	—	2	—	2	—	1	1	—	—	—	—	6	—
A. Bradock	—	2	2	—	—	1	—	—	—	—	—	5	1.2
Lewis	—	1	1	—	3	—	—	—	—	—	—	5	—
West	—	1	2	—	1	1	—	—	—	—	—	5	—
Hale	—	1	—	2	—	1	—	—	1	—	—	5	—
Barton	1	—	—	2	1	—	—	—	—	—	—	4	1.0
Laroux	1	2	—	—	—	—	1	—	—	—	—	4	—
Brown	—	—	—	—	4	—	—	—	—	—	—	4	—
Troop	—	1	—	1	—	1	1	—	—	—	—	4	—
Parsons	—	—	—	1	1	—	—	—	2	—	—	4	—
May	—	1	—	—	1	—	—	—	1	—	—	3	0.7
T. Bradock	—	—	—	—	—	1	—	1	—	—	—	2	—
Kyser	—	—	—	—	—	1	—	—	—	1	—	2	—
Hoover	1	—	—	—	—	—	1	—	—	—	—	2	—
Scott	—	—	—	—	—	—	—	—	1	—	—	2	—
Marcy	—	—	—	1	1	—	—	—	—	—	—	2	—
Goodman	1	1	—	—	—	—	—	—	—	—	—	2	—
Henry	—	—	—	—	—	1	—	—	—	—	—	1	0.2
Rio	—	—	—	—	1	—	—	—	—	—	—	1	—
Goode	—	—	—	—	—	—	—	—	1	—	—	1	—
C. Downs	—	—	—	—	1	—	—	—	—	—	—	1	—
Lively	—	—	—	1	—	—	—	—	—	—	—	1	—
Driver	1	—	—	—	—	—	—	—	—	—	—	1	—
Sub-total												418	
Other												199	
No Response or Don't Know												1003	

* Problems:
  I. Better Housing Facilities.
  II. Financial and Job Security.
  III. Better Facilities and Academic Standards in Schools.
  IV. Better Recreation Facilities.
  V. Desegregation of the Schools.
  VI. Desegregation of Other Local Facilities.
  VII. Better Communication with White Community.
  VIII. More Community Spirit and Participation.
  IX. More Political Participation.
  X. Better Medical Facilities.
  XI. Other Problems—better streets, school transportation, street lighting, etc.
** Percentages are based on sub-total of 418 responses naming individual leaders.

These minority respondents selected 42 individuals as "issue leaders" and 49 as "power leaders," with most names appearing on both lists. The issue leaders and the number of selections they received for each of ten chosen issues are listed in Table 4. Some 61.8 per cent of those queried gave "I don't know" or no responses. Names of individual leaders were provided in 25.8 per cent of the responses, and in 12.3 per cent names of organizations, neighbors, and working associates were provided in place of names of actual community leaders. It should be noted, therefore, that the percentages shown in Table 4 are based upon the 418 selections that were made of individuals perceived as leaders.

The 6 men receiving the largest number of nominations as "issue leaders" obtained votes in 8 to 10 of the problems discussed with informants. Four persons were mentioned in 5 to 6 problem areas, and 14 were mentioned as leaders in 3 to 4 areas. The ten top names on the issue-leader list received 63 per cent of the total votes cast for individual leaders in each of the 10 problems, although they made up only 23.8 per cent of all nominees. A consistent pattern rarely appeared in the selection of individual leaders for specific issues.

One exception is the 14 votes cast for Roger Hopkins as a leader in the area of recreation. Hopkins is the director of the Crescent City Negro recreation program. It is by virtue of his position that he was identified with this sub-community issue, for he received no votes in other areas. On the other hand, Banks, Alder, and French, all members of the Mayor's Commission on Race Relations—established specifically to improve communications between the races—received few votes as leaders on that issue. Wareman and Hale, both of whom have been active in procuring jobs for Negroes, received fewer mentions in this area than other leaders. Adams, who in 1950 led the litigation for adequate school facilities, received only a few more votes on this issue than others not directly involved in the battle. Similar comparisons can be made. It could be concluded, then, that the sub-community does not define its leadership in terms of specialized issues.

In an attempt to test this assumption, I made two analyses. In one I compared the sub-community "issue leaders" with the power nominees selected in the Negro leadership poll; in the second I compared these issue leaders with the power nominees selected in the sub-community poll. I first divided the leader list obtained from the leadership poll into three categories based on the sociometric positions of the leaders—top power nominees, sub-power nominees, and lesser leaders. Employing these three categories, I was able to determine what proportion of the sub-community issue nominations fell into each division.

As shown in Table 5, 41.6 per cent of those responding selected individuals falling within the sociometric category of top power nominee. Twenty-five per cent chose sub-power nominees or lesser leaders, and the remaining 33.4 per cent named random groups of individuals—organizations, neighbors, friends, or fellow workers. In 8 of the problem areas, the top power nominees received a higher proportion of the votes.

Of special interest is the breakdown of "issue leader" selections by class. Slightly over 51 per cent of the upper-class informants named leaders who appeared as power figures in the sociometric scale. Over 42 per cent of the middle class and 19.6 per cent of the lower class selected as "issue leaders" persons in the top power category. Sub-power nominees and lesser leaders were named by 26.5 per cent of the upper class, 25.1 per cent of the middle class, and 22.4 per cent of the lower class. Among the lower-class respondents, 57.9 per cent made random selections— organizations, friends, neighbors—as compared to 32.7

TABLE 5
"ISSUE LEADER" CHOICES OF SUB-COMMUNITY SAMPLE POLL, BY TYPE OF LEADER

PROBLEMS OR ISSUES**

Type of Leader	I T*	I %	II T	II %	III T	III %	IV T	IV %	V T	V %	VI T	VI %	VII T	VII %	VIII T	VIII %	IX T	IX %	X T	X %	XI T	XI %	Totals T	Totals %*
Top Power Nominee	46	48.4	65	48.0	27	41.6	12	16.2	26	50.0	20	43.5	34	58.6	5	14.3	17	39.5	6	50.0	1	14.3	259	41.6
Sub-Power Nominee	10	10.5	20	15.0	4	6.1	4	5.4	7	13.4	8	17.4	7	12.1	4	11.4	1	2.3	1	8.3	2	28.6	68	10.9
Lesser Leader	11	11.5	11	8.0	11	16.9	27	36.5	6	11.5	9	19.6	4	6.8	4	11.4	4	9.3			1	14.3	88	14.1
Neighbor	11	11.5	7	5.0	9	13.9	22	29.7	3	5.8	3	6.5	8	13.7	8	22.9	6	14.0			2	28.6	79	12.7
Friend or Family Member	3	3.1	3	2.0			4	5.4	1	1.9					3	8.6	5	11.6	1	8.3			20	3.2
Other	14	15.0	30	22.0	14	21.5	5	6.8	9	17.4	6	13.0	5	8.8	11	31.4	10	23.3	4	33.4	1	14.3	109	17.5
No Response	211		304		101		64		46		50		56		29		21		72		43		997	
Sub-total		100.0		100.0		100.0		100.0		10.00		100.0		100.0		100.0		100.0		100.0		100.0		100.0
Minus No Response	95		136		65		74		52		46		58		35		43		12		7		623	
Grand Total	306		440		166		138		98		96		114		64		64		84		50		1620	

* T equals Total votes cast; % equals the percentage of votes cast, minus the no responses, for each problem or issue.
** See code numbers at bottom of Table 4 to identify problems or issues.

per cent of the middle class and 22.5 per cent of the upper class.

I then turned to the Negro community's selection of power and influence leaders, to make further comparisons with its issue leader selections. Respondents were asked to list the five Negroes whom they considered the most influential. Table 6 shows the percentage of votes each received. Of the 1415 votes cast, 48 per cent were residuals or no responses, and 52 per cent were nominations for individual leaders. Of these, 33 per cent were cast for six of the twelve leaders who appeared as top power nominees among the sociometric selections of the Negro leadership poll. By examining the 732 votes cast for the 49 nominees, we find that 64.2 per cent were cast for men who appeared as top power nominees, 18 per cent for sub-power nominees, and 11.3 per cent for lesser leaders.

Nearly 65 per cent of the upper class, 54.9 per cent of the middle class and 27.4 per cent of the lower class voted for leaders who appeared as top power nominees in the Negro leadership poll. Sub-power nominees received 16.5 per cent of the upper-class votes, 11.1 per cent of the middle-class votes, and 13.1 per cent of the lower-class votes in the community sample. Lower-class informants gave residual categories 41.2 per cent of their votes, while only 14 per cent of the upper-class and 12.8 per cent of the middle-class votes were distributed in these categories. It is apparent, then, that upper- and middle-class respondents tended to choose leaders from the sociometric power and sub-power categories more frequently than did lower-class respondents. This was also the case in the selection of issue leaders.

Tables 4 and 6 show that respondents selected the same individuals as issue leaders that they selected as power leaders. Some 92.8 per cent of the issue leader choices and 79.5 per cent of the power leader choices are the same.

TABLE 6

NEGRO LEADERS RANKED ACCORDING TO NUMBER OF
VOTES RECEIVED AS POWER NOMINEES, BY
SUB-COMMUNITY SAMPLE

Leader	Number of Votes	Percent of Leader Responses*
Adams	122	16.7
McDonald	102	13.9
Karns	73	10.0
Banks	61	8.3
Alder	45	6.1
French, Kyser	31	4.2
Swanson	24	3.3
Healy	19	2.6
T. Downs	16	2.2
Wareman	15	2.1
A. Bradock, Hoover, Jackson, R. Johnson, Marshall	12	1.6
T. Bradock, Smith	10	1.4
Hale, Driver, Miller	9	1.2
West, Sherwood, Parsons	7	1.0
Erickson, Arthur	6	0.8
Hopkins, Laroux, Goodman, Nelson, Troop, Alston	4	0.5
Lewis, Conners, Simmons, Barton	3	0.4
Carver, May, Dart, C. Downs	2	0.3
Goode, Lively, Green, Henry, Rio, Marcy, Sandy, Baker, Merrit	1	0.1
Sub-total	732	
Other	126	
No Response or Don't Know	557	

* Percentages based on sub-total of 732 responses naming individual leaders.

Eight of the top 12 selections correspond on each list, and 20 of the first 25 correspond.

The Spearman rank correlation coefficient used to test for *rho* among 20 mutual selections gave a value equal to .655 with the correction factor T taken into account for tied groupings. The following null hypothesis was tested: the two variables of leadership studied in the sub-community—"issue" and "power"—are not associated. The observed value of *rho* differs from zero only by chance. It was found, using the t distribution, that t was equal to 3.68.

With 18 degrees of freedom, the probability of a *t* as large as 3.68 was less than .01, but greater than .001. The null hypothesis could therefore be rejected, for there was a significant positive association between the rank of the 20 top issue leader and power leader nominations in the sub-community at the .01 level of significance.[7]

Similar reasons were given by the community sample respondents for selecting both their issue leaders and power nominees. In addition, such reasons corresponded very closely to those given by the Negro leader respondents— that is, institutional position; personal characteristics; and civic service within the community.

To complete the picture of the reputed sub-community leaders, the investigation moved to a third group of informants—the white leaders of Crescent City. Using an abbreviated form of the chain-referral technique for identifying leaders, the author interviewed twenty of the sociometric white top power and sub-power leaders.[8]

The leadership structure of Crescent City's white community has been regarded as fluid—changing from generation to generation as new and younger men take over positions of responsibility. However, the presence of some "old" families which have been in power since the end of

7. For formulas used, see Sidney Siegel, *Nonparametric Statistics* (New York: McGraw-Hill Book Company, Inc., 1956), pp. 206-13.

$r_s = 1 - \dfrac{6\Sigma D^2}{N(N^2 - 1)}$. The formula $t = r_s \sqrt{\dfrac{N-2}{1-r_s}}$ was used for $N > 10$, as discussed in Siegel.

8. The rating of the white leaders interviewed is based on their sociometric rank in a broader study of urban centers in the Middle South. Those interviewed for the purposes of this study are a representative sample of the 37 individuals who appeared as upper- and lower-limits leaders in the broader study. Of the top 21 power leaders in this broader study, 8 represented business and finance, 5 represented commerce, 1 represented industry, 2 represented the professions, 4 represented politics, and 1 represented civic endeavor and leisure—very close to the breakdown for the 20 persons interviewed in this study.

the nineteenth century has provided a measure of stability. Leadership is predominantly in the hands of representatives of financial and commercial enterprises in the white community. And one of the questions dividing the white leaders is whether to diversify the industrial and economic base or to maintain the economic status quo.

The researcher moved from leader to leader as each was mentioned by others.[9] The first respondent was a professional man, active in civic affairs and known to be fairly liberal in his racial attitudes. Of those interviewed, eight men were connected with banking, insurance, and finance, one was an industrial executive, and four (including the mayor) were owners and presidents of large commercial enterprises. The professions were represented by two attorneys, one highly placed college administrator, and the minister of the most influential white upper-class church. One respondent (an attorney) was an active political party chairman; another was a senator in the state legislature. Two of the respondents were women, one of whom was from an old and wealthy Crescent City family and has devoted much of her time to community philanthropies, civic affairs, and politics. The second woman was the wife of a surgeon and was also active in civic and religious affairs, as well as race relations.

The leaders interviewed ranged in age from thirty-two to sixty-nine, with a mean age of fifty. They have lived in Crescent City an average of 31.1 years, and 49 per cent were born in Mid-South State. Five of the white leaders contacted were associated with one of the several business enterprises controlled by the Jackson A. Vale family, and they and others associated with the numerous Vale firms were often referred to collectively as the "Vale group."

9. For a discussion of this technique, see Robert Dahl, "Hierarchy, Democracy and Bargaining in Politics and Economics," in *Research Frontiers in Politics and Government* (Washington, D.C.: Brookings Institution, 1955), pp. 50-53.

Other such groups were somewhat harder to distinguish. A few respondents mentioned those individuals associated with the Cranston family enterprises, but several others suggested that Roger Cranston and his associates had been losing influence because of their ultra-conservative approach to industrial development and labor and race relations. A maverick group of very conservative, anti-Negro citizens joined together for political reasons in 1957, but it is difficult to determine how closely, if at all, the Cranston family was affiliated with this group, though these conservatives did support the candidacy of a Cranston family member for mayor in 1958. He was defeated by the incumbent Murphy with the backing of the Vale family as well as Negro leaders.

Thirty individuals from the minority community were identified by the white leadership as members of the Negro power elite. The number of votes received by each is recorded in Table 7. An average of 7.2 persons were mentioned by each white informant; a total of 146 nominations were made. Of these, 92 of the votes, or 63 per cent, were cast for 8 individuals, or 26.6 per cent of those nominated. The remaining 37 per cent of the votes went to 22 persons, or 73.4 per cent of those mentioned as top Negro leaders. As was true of the results of the Negro leader poll, 5 of the top 7 Negroes selected were economic dominants in the sub-community. Three of the 10 top-ranking Negroes selected by white leaders may be regarded as conservative, 3 as moderate, and 4 as liberal in their approaches to race relations and civil rights, according to their Negro-leader peers. In making their selections, white leaders gave great weight to the formal institutional positions held by Negroes. White leaders were, as well, torn between selecting those Negroes who they felt were really most powerful and those whom they believed to be more acceptable to the white leadership. Sev-

TABLE 7
NEGRO LEADERS RANKED ACCORDING TO NUMBER
OF VOTES RECEIVED AS POWER NOMINEES, BY
WHITE LEADERSHIP POLL

Leaders	Number of votes received
Banks, Alder	16
McDonald	15
Adams	14
French	10
Karns	8
A. Bradock	7
T. Bradock	6
Erickson, Wareman	5
Healy, Hale	4
Hoover, Sherwood, Miller, Driver, Marshall, Kyser	3
Williams, Nelson, Pace, Smith, Ross, Swanson	2
Hughes, Troop, Arthur, Jackson, Whitting, Black	1

eral indicated that Alder was the top leader and "most influential among the whites because he was of the 'old school'—ambitious but not liberal." Others felt that Banks was the most acceptable leader. One informant said that he wished Banks were the most powerful leader among the Negroes, though he acknowledged that there were others more influential in the sub-community.

One man, Oscar Ford, made his nominations by listing first those Negroes most acceptable to the average white leader, then those he sensed were most influential among the Negroes. According to him, Banks, French, Alder, Ruth Johnson, and Kyser were the leading Negroes approved by the whites. He identified Adams, McDonald, Wareman, Hoover, Healy, Sherwood, Marshall, and Hale as the actual powers in the sub-community, and Adams as the most powerful in this group. He also identified Art Troop, a radical young Negro leader with a following among some of the younger sub-community members, especially the college students, as one who might eventually challenge the Negro "old guard." Ford is one of the most active members of the Mayor's Race Relations Commission, but feels he has yet to reach the real Negro policy- and decision-makers.

Five whites avowed that Adams was too liberal, and several commented that they had feared McDonald would be too aggressive when he was elected to the City Council (they had feared the same of Banks previously). Most agreed that thus far McDonald had been very "level-headed." (The more personal association individual white leaders had with individual Negro leaders, the greater tendency there was for the Negroes to be held in favorable regard). Mayor Murphy strongly emphasized that none of the Negro leaders in Crescent City was radical. Nor did he believe, on the other hand, that any of the top men, including Alder, French, Banks, and T. Bradock, were "accommodating." "For a Negro leader to be accommodating in this day and age would mean a loss of any support or influence he might have."

J. Arthur Vale, Jr., analyzed the Negro power structure in terms of three institutional groups of power figures— the economic elite led by Karns, Alder, and Adams; the political elite surrounding McDonald ("although there may be others calling the plays"); and the educational elite, made up of various influential members of the faculty and administration at Mid-South College for Negroes.

There seemed to be genuine respect for Negro leaders among a majority of the white informants, however grudgingly it was admitted. Even so, the respondents exhibited reluctance to associate themselves actively with overt attempts to improve relationships between the races for fear of "what the others would think." A few of the older white leaders confided that "something must be done to improve things between the races in Crescent City." A statement by Richard Bosworth, president of the Piedmont National Bank (part of the Vale family interests), typifies the covert sentiment. "Southern Life, the People's State Bank, and one or two other Negro groups need to have 25 to 30 members in our Chamber of Commerce," said Bosworth. "Now I'm not a 'Nigra lover,' but we have to face cold-blooded facts, and things are moving too slowly. Southern Life is our largest locally owned firm, and they should be included."

When the results of the three polls had been tabulated, my investigation moved to a comparative analysis. I began by studying the relationship between the power leader selections of the Negro leadership poll and the sub-community poll. A significant agreement was observed in the leadership rankings of these two groups. Altogether, 89.3 per cent (25 out of 28 selections) of the Negro leadership poll selections and 51 per cent (25 out of 49 selections) of the sub-community poll selections corresponded. As reported, 94 per cent of the votes cast for power leaders in the sub-community sample were accorded to individuals who appeared as power nominees in the Negro leadership poll—that is, to the 25 mutual selections.

Using the Spearman rank correlation coefficient to test for the association of the rankings of mutually selected names, r_s was found to equal .73, with the correction factor T taken into account for tied groupings. The null hypothesis that the observed value of *rho* occurred by chance and that the two variables under study were not associated was tested. By utilizing the t test, I found that the probability of observing an r_s of 173 was $t = 5.12$. The probability of such a value of t with 23 degrees of freedom was less than .001. The null hypothesis was therefore rejected and the conclusion was reached that there was a significant positive association between the rankings of the

25 mutual selections of the Negro leader informants and the sub-community sample informants.

I next turned to an analysis of the Negro leadership rankings made by all three groups of informants. Seventy-five per cent (21 out of 28 selections) of the Negro leader selections, 43 per cent (21 out of 49 nominations) of the sub-community selections, and 70 per cent (21 out of 30 nominations) of the white leader selections were matched. In order to test the association between the three sets of rankings, the Kendall coefficient of concordance *W* was utilized.[10]

The coefficient of concordance *W* had a value of .76 when the correctional factor *T* was taken into account for tied groupings. To find the significance of the observed value of *W,* the null hypothesis that the three sets of rankings were independent or unrelated was tested. The significance of $W = .76$ was tested by χ^2. It was found that the value of *chi* square was 45.6 (with 20 degrees of freedom), which is significant beyond the .001 level. Therefore the null hypothesis was rejected, and it was concluded that the agreement among the three sets of rankings was significantly higher than could be expected from chance variation.

Of the three groups that ranked Negro leaders in the power attribution method, the sub-community sample contained the largest number of nominees who failed to appear on either of the other two lists. There were 18 such names submitted by the sub-community sample, or 36.7 per cent of the total number of individuals nominated. It is important to note, however, that this group of nominees

10. See Siegel, *Nonparametric Statistics,* pp. 229-39; M. G. Kendall, *Rank Correlation Methods* (London: Griffin, 1948). The formulas used are:

$$W = \frac{s}{\frac{1}{12}k^2(N^3 - N) - k\sum_T T} \quad \text{and} \quad \chi^2 = k(N-1)W.$$

received only 7.6 per cent of the total number of votes cast by sub-community respondents, making the agreement among the three groups even more striking. The white-leader informants nominated 6 individuals not mentioned by either of the Negro informant groups. These persons received only 6.2 per cent of the total white-leader vote.

It might, perhaps, have been expected that the selections of the two groups of Negro informants would show substantial agreement, but the agreement between the selections of white and Negro respondents was surprising. Unlike the research results in other southern urban centers, Crescent City results indicate that the white leadership there does have knowledge about those Negroes *reputed* to have power and influence. There are several explanations for this phenomenon. The similarity in the historical development of the socio-economic structure of the two racial groups is one. The higher educational, social, and occupational status of the Negro leadership of Crescent City is another. The effectiveness of Crescent City's top minority leaders in gaining access to positions of power and in influencing decisions in both racial communities also has a bearing. It is possible, too, that more and wider channels of communication exist between the two racial groups in Crescent City and, for that matter, that power is not exerted behind the scenes to as great an extent as is sometimes believed.

Dahl has laid down the principle that the researcher, using a variety of techniques for uncovering leadership, can expect to find a high correlation between findings in a highly integrated community with a persistent or traditional leadership group.[11] At this point it is appropriate only to speculate on the amount of integration to be found in Crescent City's Negro population. Certainly, as noted

11. Dahl, "Hierarchy, Democracy and Bargaining in Politics and Economics," in *Research Frontiers*, pp. 50-57.

in chapter III, extensive economic, educational, religious, and occupational differences do exist in the sub-community. At the upper- and middle-class levels, however, integration is more obvious. Institutional organizations in Crescent City may also be more highly integrated than they are in other communities. This may particularly be true of the present-day political and economic organizations.

We observed in chapter III that there is a "traditional" or persistent leadership, especially among the economic dominants. In general, however, the leadership structure has become much more fluid over the years, though a pattern of "grooming" promising younger men for leadership does exist. Many of the power attribution nominees have assumed positions of leadership through their own efforts, without benefit of family influence.

Many avenues to leadership that are open to white citizens are, of course, blocked to Negroes. Thus the leadership base is narrow, and the leaders develop in a limited institutional and organizational setting. The articulate, educated class is small, and the leadership base is narrow in this sense, as well. It is quite possible, then, that accurate knowledge of the top Negro leaders is relatively easy to obtain by both Negro and white, for minority power leaders have a restricted but *distinctive* number of sources from which to emerge.

While it is not possible on the evidence I have cited to establish a hierarchy of power among the top Negro leaders in Crescent City (indeed, it may be impossible to do so at any time for any community), some sociometric classification is possible. Thirty-one individuals obtained the greatest proportion (arbitrarily established as 3 or more votes in at least 2 of the 3 leadership polls) of nominations as power figures. The voting for these 31 is tallied in Table 8. Other leaders may appear in this study briefly

TABLE 8

NEGRO LEADERS LISTED BY NUMBER OF VOTES RECEIVED
FROM THREE LEADERSHIP POLLS, AS POWER NOMINEES

Leaders	Negro Leader Votes	White Leader Votes	Sub-Community Votes	Totals
Howard T. Adams	44	14	122	180
M. Steven McDonald	49	15	102	166
I. N. Karns	27	8	73	108
Nathan Banks	26	16	61	103
Silas Alder	18	16	45	79
Albert French	12	10	31	53
Robert Healy	18	4	19	41
Allen Kyser	7	3	31	41
N. B. Swanson	3	2	24	29
Charles Wareman	6	5	15	26
William C. Hoover	9	3	12	24
Alice Bradock	4	7	12	23
T. O. Bradock	6	6	10	22
David Hale	7	4	9	20
H. I. Erickson	8	5	6	19
O. G. Sherwood	7	3	7	17
John Miller	5	3	9	17
Thomas Marshall	1	3	12	16
D. E. Jackson	3	1	12	16
Charles Driver	2	3	9	14
Ruth Johnson	2	–	12	14
Ellwood Smith	2	2	10	14
S. T. Parsons	1	–	7	8
Winston Arthur	–	1	6	7
R. E. Laroux	2	–	4	6
Fred Nelson	–	2	4	6
Art Troop	–	1	4	5
Jack Simmons	1	–	3	4
Stanley Lewis	1	–	3	4
Miles Conners	1	–	3	4
Charles May	1	–	2	3
TOTALS	273	137	679	1089

in a minor role, but it is a majority of those in this group of 31 that are omnipresent in the currents of Crescent City's organizational life.

For comparative purposes the 31 power nominees were again divided into two groups, *top power nominees* and *sub-power nominees*. These categories are arbitrary, too, for there can be no line between one type of leader and the

other.   However, it is significant that the top 10 sociometric leaders—those receiving 25 or more votes—received 74.5 per cent of the total number of votes cast for
the 31 power nominees.

Of the group of 31, only two were women. This con-
trasts with Barth's findings in a West Coast Negro community, where 44 per cent of the 36 top leaders were
women, but coincides with Hunter's research in Regional
City. Neither of the two women among Crescent City's
Negro leaders was a power leader.

A summary of selected social characteristics is recorded
in Table 9.   The leaders ranged in age from thirty-one to
eighty-one, with the mean age of 53.7.   The top power nominees tend to be older than the sub-power nominees and
have, on the average, resided in Crescent City 9 years
longer than the sub-power nominees.   One of the top power
nominees had no formal education; three attended, but
did not complete, college; the others were college graduates.   All but two of the sub-power nominees attended
college.   In the total group of reputed power leaders, 19
had taken graduate work.   Ninety per cent of the top power
nominees were affiliated with upper-class churches, in contrast to 44.4 per cent of the sub-power nominees, and a
majority of the 31 leaders were on their church governing
boards either at the state or national level.   All leaders
were property owners.   Five of them owned business
property in addition to rental property and residences.

The leaders' occupations (Table 10) locate them in
the institutional structure of Crescent City's sub-community.

Most of the leaders held responsible positions. They
were fairly evenly distributed between business and the
professions.   Only 22.6 per cent of the leaders were self-
employed, as owners or managers of small businesses or
as professionals.   The remainder were salaried employees
of the larger firms. Eleven of the 31 leaders were in bank-

TABLE 9

SOCIAL CHARACTERISTICS OF THIRTY-ONE TOP POWER
AND SUB-POWER NOMINEES IN CRESCENT CITY
SUB-COMMUNITY

Characteristics	Top Power Nominees	Sub-Power Nominees	Totals For Group
Age: Mean Years	58.1	51.4	53.7
Place of Birth:			
Mid-South State	40.0%	47.4%	44.8%
Other Southern States	60.0%	47.4%	51.7%
Outside South	——	5.2%	3.4%
Mean Years Residence in Crescent City	35.6	26.8	29.9
Education:			
Median Years	16.5	17.0	17.0
Mean Years	15.2	15.9	15.3
Religious Affiliation:			
Upper Class	90.0%	44.4%	60.7%
Middle Class	——	55.5%	35.7%
None	10.0%	——	3.6%
Mean Number of Local Negro Organization Memberships	4.0	4.2	4.1
Mean Number of Board of Directors Memberships	7.6	3.5	4.8
Mean Number of Biracial Association Memberships (Local, State, and National)	3.5	3.3	3.4

ing, finance, and insurance. Six of the 10 top power nominees were economic dominants. The professions were represented by 6 college administrators or faculty members, 4 attorneys, and 5 ministers. In the college, Dr. Charles Wareman has been among the most active and outspoken in community affairs. Dr. Miller, of the department of political science, has also been active and has been candidate for the City Council on three occasions.

As Table 10 indicates, Karns and Alder, as board chairman and president of Southern Life, held by far the

TABLE 10

POWER NOMINEES BY OCCUPATIONAL POSITION

Type of Occupation	Name of Leader	Name of Organization	Position Held	Number of Employees under Administrative Control
Banking, Finance, and Insurance	Adams	Farm and Home Insurance	President	35
	Alder	Southern Life Insurance	President	1200
	Arthur	People's State Bank	Chairman, Board	20
	Banks	Community Savings and Loan	Vice-President, General Manager	4
	Driver	Commercial Bank and Trust	Manager	14
	Conners	Southern Life Insurance	Senior Vice-President	350
	Karns	Southern Life Insurance	Chairman, Board	1200
	Laroux	Eastern Realty Corporation	Ex Vice-President	25
	McDonald	Peoples State Bank	Ex Vice-President	18
	Nelson	Consolidated Insurance and Realty	Treasurer	2
	Simmons	Farm & Home Insurance	Agency Director	30
Commerce and Small Business	Hale	Holis Transport Co.	Co-Owner, President	9
	Healy	Crescent Printing and Publishing Co.	Owner, Publisher	10
	Smith	Smith and Sons, Undertakers	Owner, Director	6
	Swanson	Swanson Enterprises	President	20
Professions	A. Bradock	Mid-South College	Department Chairman	5
	T. Bradock	Cowles Theological Seminary	Professor	2
	Erickson	Law firm	Corporation Lawyer	2
	French	Mid-South College	President	210
	Hoover	First Methodist Church	Minister	2
	Jackson	St. John's A.M.E. Church	Minister	6
	Johnson	Mid-South College	Dean	20
	Kyser	St. Paul's Episcopal Church	Minister, Emeritus	3
	Marshall	Law firm	Attorney	3
	Mays	Law firm	Attorney	1
	Miller	Private office	Professor	0
	Sherwood	Mid-South College	Attorney	1
	Wareman	Mid-South College	Professor	0
	Troop	Temple Baptist Church	Educational Director	1
	Parsons	Folsom St. Methodist Church	Minister	4
Labor	Lewis	United Tobacco	Chairman, Shop Committee; Vice-President, International Tobacco Workers	0

most responsible positions, in terms of the number of employees under their authority. Conners, vice-president in charge of agency directors for Southern Life, was responsible for 350 employees in Life's 27 branch offices in 10 states. Dr. French, president of Mid-South College, stood third with 210 employees. Unlike Hunter, however, this researcher found no significant correlation between the number of persons under administrative control and the leadership ranking of the individual vested with this control. Howard Adams, for example, who received the largest number of nominations as a power figure, had only 35 employees under him at Farm and Home Insurance. McDonald, Healy, Banks, and Kyser, who are among the top ten sociometric selections, all had fewer than 20 employees under their control.

The residences of Crescent City's power and sub-power nominees are clustered in the southern end of Holis district. Twenty-seven of the top 31 leaders reside in Holis or its environs—in the University Park section or on the periphery of the Park area in the upper-middle-class sections. The homes of the power nominees are among the most imposing in the Negro community. Other leaders live in rather typical middle-class homes of brick, shingle, or clapboard, away from the heavy traffic and the industrial and commercial enterprises that border Holis district. Figure 3 maps the distribution of residences of power leaders.

Although the leaders of the minority community tend to live apart from its masses (this was also Hunter's observation in Regional City), they never live far away. The upper- and middle-class sections of Holis district are surrounded on three sides by lower-class dwelling areas, some of them slums and transitional zones. One would have to close his eyes not to see the poverty that exists for so many of Crescent City's minority population—and with

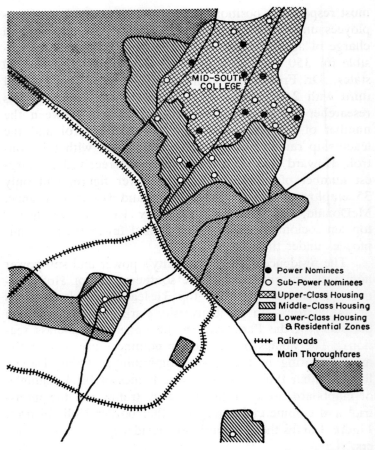

FIG. 3. Residence of top power and sub-power nominees in Crescent City, by class.

a few exceptions the Negro leadership does not close its eyes.

The composite list of power and sub-power nominees, when it was finally compiled, was employed as a tentative guide to further exploration. Because of the high incidence of agreement found among the three groups of respondents,

I regarded the list with some confidence. By observing the behavior of the power and sub-power nominees in the decision-making process, I attempted next to develop a more definitive picture of their places in the power structure. Specifically, I would to this end trace the behavior of Negro leaders as it was revealed in selected community activities and issues, and from this phase of the investigation I hoped to discover who *actually* wielded power in the sub-community, in distinction to who was *reputed* to wield power.

CHAPTER V

LEADERSHIP IN ACTION: THE
DYNAMIC PROCESSES OF POWER

INVESTIGATION of concrete issues and decisions in the Crescent sub-community provided a necessary refinement to the list of leaders resulting from the polls. By identifying active participants in decision-making, it helped to narrow the original list of power nominees. It also established more surely the importance of the roles of certain individuals. This more dynamic investigation of activities uncovered, as well, a significant change taking place in the character of Crescent City Negro leadership and its policies, especially since 1954.

As was suggested in chapter IV, all individuals playing key roles in issues appeared among the 31 power nominees. The reverse, however, was not true. Not all of those who were nominated as leaders were found to play such key decision-making roles.

In order to identify issues considered salient by both Negroes and whites, data were obtained from newspaper accounts (1957 to 1960), interview materials from whites and Negroes, attendance at committee and organizational meetings, special policy statements, and organizational reports. In addition, both the sub-community leaders and the informants in the sub-community sample poll were asked to reveal what they considered the three basic problems of the Negro community. Their replies are registered in Table 11, by issue and number of votes.

No attempt was made to include white leaders in my discussion of issues, except as it was necessary to do so to understand the patterns of interaction between the two racial groups. Many of the white and Negro leaders were involved in a wide variety of issues—Negroes perhaps more than whites. Both whites and Negroes commonly implemented their policies through two or three key organizations. Both tended to call upon less influential associations and individuals for actual execution of their projects.

TABLE 11

MAJOR ISSUE AREAS FACING SUB-COMMUNITY AS REPORTED BY NEGRO LEADER AND SUB-COMMUNITY POLLS, BY NUMBER OF VOTES

Issue Areas	Sub-Community Votes	Negro Leader Votes
Economic	374	51
Education	132	26
Intergroup-Interrace Relations	106	18
All Other Issues	201	28
No Response	36	24
TOTALS	849*	147**

* Based on three selections of 283 respondents.
** Based on three selections of 49 respondents.

The white leaders were most concerned with economic problems and community expansion. Their interests, however, did cut into political, educational, civic, and religious issues. Negroes were also concerned with economic problems, but their activity in this area was partially blocked by their minority status. Most Negroes define the whole desegregation issue in terms of an avenue toward greater economic opportunities.

The "reactionary" segment of white leadership, which directs the white efforts to prevent or discourage needed change in Crescent City, has progressively lost power and influence. While there is no certainty that this trend will continue, it has benefited the Negro community in recent years.

Perhaps the basic issue in Crescent City has been the need for diversification of the economic base. Negro leadership has been in sympathy with the progressive elements of the white community leading the fight for projects calculated to expand and vary the city's economic base. When the Committee for Industrial and Economic Expansion was organized, membership in it was extended to a few leaders of the Negro community—Adams, Karns, Banks, Alder, Laroux, McDonald, and French. Many projects— the development of an industrial research park, for instance—engendered little controversy. Negro leaders simply gave their support. Because the Negro holds the balance of voting power in Crescent City, however, Negro leaders gradually tied their support more and more to conditions, even on issues not themselves controversial. And when an issue was clearly controversial, Negro leaders went immediately into action. The Industrial Education Center is a case in point.

In February, 1958, the state legislature set up a budget for four Industrial Education Centers as part of a program to bring in new industry. Progressive white leaders of the Crescent community saw in the Centers a means of furthering their own program of economic development. They began to lay plans to acquire one of the Centers for Crescent City. The more conservative elements were not interested. Some individuals merely opposed "another bond issue." Negro leaders, however, viewed the establishment of a Center in Crescent City as a progressive step in the economic development of their people.

Jack Vale III formed an all-white committee to get the project under way. Working closely with the project were

state senator Guy Stratton, Vale Cort, Jr., Richard Bosworth, Mayor Murphy, and Grant Bond of the Chamber
of Commerce. They took the plan before the Committee
for Industrial and Economic Expansion, the Chamber of
Commerce, the Merchants Association, and the leaders of
the Crescent Negro Council. All favored the plan.

Once the preliminary stage was past, Vale turned to
the school administrators for help. In March, 1958, a
survey was undertaken by the administrations of the city
and county schools to determine the need for the Center.
Eventually, the Crescent school board agreed to submit an
application for an Industrial Education Center. The application was approved, providing that the necessary bond
issue passed.

In July, 1958, Nathan Banks, a Negro member of the
school board, asked what provision the board was making
for Negro participation in the Center's services. Edward
Fulton, chairman of the Board and a corporation lawyer
for the Central Textiles Company, indicated that, as far
as the school board was concerned, current educational
policies would prevail. The board assumed that it would
control teacher employment and student admission practices on a "white only" basis.

At this stage of the project, the Negro leaders, alerted
by Banks, stepped in, determined to have a voice in the
use of the Center. Banks knew that the policy that the
school board anticipated applying might mean the defeat
of the bond issue upon which the establishment of the
Crescent City Center depended, and he so informed the
Crescent Negro Council and Jack Vale III. On July 10,
1958, Vale called Harris Erickson of the Crescent Negro
Council and, referring to the school board's position, inquired what the chances were for Negro backing on the
bond issue if that position were allowed to stand. When
Erickson indicated that Negro backing would be doubtful,

Vale suggested a meeting of white and Negro leaders. Erickson promised he would do what he could.

The next day Erickson had lunch at the Beta Dining Room with Jack Simmons of the Farm and Home Insurance Company and mentioned Vale's request for a meeting. As the two men talked, Howard Adams walked by. At their request, Adams joined them for a moment to discuss the Industrial Education Center project. Adams advised that it would be wise to get an informal committee together for policy talks and declared that he would contact two or three other Negro leaders to serve on the committee along with himself, Erickson, and Simmons. He called Steven McDonald, the Negro member of the City Council, and David Hale, president of the Negro Business League and chairman of the Economic Committee of the Crescent Negro Council. The following week Adams, Erickson, Hale, and McDonald met with Vale's committee in Vale's office in the Great Southern State Bank building. Simmons was away from the city on business at this initial meeting, but was present at several subsequent meetings.

When the Negro leaders left the first meeting, they had indicated that a segregated policy in the Industrial Education Center would result in the loss of their support of the bond issue. Other joint meetings of the white and Negro committees followed. Separate conferences were held between Vale and Adams, or Vale, Hale, and Simmons. In these later meetings, Negro leaders set forth their views on policies acceptable to them. A few Negro leaders told the Economic Committee of the Negro Council they were willing to go along with the Industrial Center project in the hope that it would eventually be desegregated. Adams and McDonald, however, were unwilling to force acceptance of a segregated Center on the Council. Finally, Adams agreed to hold up action by the Negro Council on the question of policy on the bond issue until Vale's committee could negotiate with other white organizations to develop a liberal policy.

Vale and a committee of associates went to work to save the Center. In August they distributed a memorandum to all agencies involved, suggesting three possible approaches: admission of whites only; admission of both white and Negro adults, but on a segregated basis; and admission of white and Negro adults on a non-segregated basis, but with a continuance of segregation in vocational education for high school students.

The memorandum explained the probable consequence of the first two approaches—Negro opposition and the defeat of the project. Vale and his committee went on record as favoring the third approach. They urged those to whom the memo was sent to discuss the matter and to inform the committee what their attitudes were.

Vale next contacted key white leaders personally. One man he had to convince was Richard Yancy, chairman of the Committee for Industrial and Economic Expansion, president of the Union Industrial Machinery Company, and a strong segregationist. Vale was able to persuade Yancy that there was no alternative to integration of the Industrial Education Center. From this point on, Vale relied on Yancy to persuade other conservative leaders of the community.

Vale, Cort, Bosworth, and several other white leaders began meeting early in September, 1958, to frame final policies, taking into consideration the suggestions obtained from both whites and Negroes. At this time it was decided that the Center would be administered by the Crescent City school board, under regulations of the State Board of Education, but that it would not be regarded as an integral part of the city school system since attendance would be entirely voluntary. Only adult males would be eligible for attendance. The Center would serve as a regional facility for industrial education, with students from outside the city being charged a reasonable tuition. Industrial studies given in city high schools would continue to be segregated. The State Board of Education would assume the direct expenses of the Center. The primary responsibility of the local school board would be to provide facilities for the Center and administrative supervision of its operation, while the Center, in turn, would make advanced instruction in industrial subjects available to supplement the ordinary high school curriculum.

In restricting admission to adult males, the leaders hoped to avoid the common white opposition to integration without regard to sex. The general policies thus formulated were approved by majority and minority community leaders. Finally, Vale's committee worked out the detailed admission requirements it felt to be acceptable to both groups.

On September 12 Vale met with Simmons and informed him that an understanding with the white leaders had been reached that the Center would be integrated and that admission requirements would make no reference to race. Vale asked Simmons to confer with the other Negro leaders on the basis of this understanding prior to the bond issue vote on October 4, 1958.

The school board accepted the recommendations of Vale's committee on the day after the Vale-Simmons meeting and announced its admissions policy to the press. According to that policy, applicants for admission to the Center must be not less than eighteen years of age, or they must be high school graduates; they must score no less than 95 on a standard intelligence test; they must have successfully completed no less than eight units of high school work or the equivalent; they must be of good moral character and furnish at least three satisfactory character references;

they must be capable of doing the work for which they are being trained; and they must be able to meet such other admission requirements as are prescribed for each course of study by the State Board of Education.

When Jack Simmons called Howard Adams the morning of September 13 to report on his meeting with Vale, Adams suggested that Simmons call a joint meeting of the Crescent Negro Council Economic and Education Committees. He then contacted other interested persons. Adams, McDonald, Hale, Erickson, Simmons, Peter Martin, Jr., J. A. Bronton, Tom Marshall, and Fred Nelson met at the Natchez Club on the evening of September 17, 1958. McDonald proposed that the joint committees present a favorable report to the Crescent Negro Council. He said that he had no doubt the white leaders fully intended to carry out their promises. Erickson, Simmons, Bronton, and Martin agreed, pointing out also that if Crescent City voted against the Center it would be located in a community in the eastern part of the state, where Negroes would hardly have any chance of being admitted.

Hale, Nelson, and Marshall did not agree, believing that with the Crescent school board in charge of admission there was no assurance that a desegrated program would be carried out. Hale moved that, in view of the absence of a clear non-discriminatory clause, the joint committees ask for defeat of the bond issue.

Adams' opinion was divided. He said he would go along with the majority, but he tended to agree with Hale on the necessity for a positive commitment. He informed the joint committees that if their report met any disapproval he would not push for its acceptance by the Council as a whole. The committees finally moved that the Council recommend that Negro citizens support the bond issue for the Center and that the Council make a special effort to find at least ten qualified Negroes to apply for admission to the Center.

Seventy-five persons were in attendance when the full Crescent Negro Council met the following evening. Adams called for the Industrial Center report, and the first of the two motions met with immediate opposition. Tom Marshall, Conrad May, Bob Healy, O. G. Sherwood, Charles Driver, S. T. Parsons, William Hoover, David Hale, Stanley Lewis, and Charles Wareman spoke in opposition to supporting the bond issue without a definite statement on integration.

The first motion was defeated by majority vote. An alternative motion by Driver was passed. It stated, in effect, that without a definite committment to non-discrimination, the Crescent Negro Council would not support the bond issue.

Jack Vale III was so notified by a telephone call from Simmons the following day. Immediately Vale began to rally his forces. He called Farsworth Pennman, president of the Chamber of Commerce, and Yancy and told them that the desegregation policy would have to be explicit if necessary Negro support of the bond issue were to be obtained. Pennman and Yancy reacted favorably and promised to line up white organizational support. Vale then called in his committee, which met with the executive committee of the school board on September 19 and with the entire board on the evening of September 22.

On September 24 Vale asked Adams to arrange a meeting of Negro leaders on the following afternoon. Adams agreed. Adams, Banks, Hale, and Simmons gathered in Vale's office, and Vale informed them that he could give them positive assurance that the Center would be desegregated. Adams then advised Vale that once the assurance was made public he could be sure of Negro support. That evening the news appeared in the Crescent City papers:

"All qualified males, regardless of race, creed, or color, will be eligible to enroll in the proposed Industrial Education Center."

Charles Wareman, executive secretary of the Crescent Negro Council, contacted key individuals in the sub-community to solicit their support of the bond issue. O. G. Sherwood and Ellwood Smith talked to the precinct committeemen. Hale alerted the members of the Negro Business League. D. E. Jackson asked members of the Ministerial Council to make appropriate announcements at Sunday services. William Hoover of the N.A.A.C.P. worked with Bob Healy in getting pamphlets distributed, while Stanley Lewis reached the Negro Labor Board. Thus, from the apex of leadership the campaign moved in its final stages down through the organizational channels of the Negro community. On October 4, 1958, Crescent City's citizenry voted on the bond issue. Ballots from the Negro wards assured its passage.

Not all of the power nominees were involved in the issue. Karns and Alder, for example, took no active part. They were willing to support Adams' decisions. Nathan Banks acted as liaison between the two elements of the biracial structure, attempting to discover and define the stumbling blocks that might keep the Center from becoming a reality. Bob Healey and O. G. Sherwood did not at first commit themselves. They and a few of the younger and more militant leaders were on the minds of the other Negro leaders as decisions were being made, and their influence was partly responsible for the final decision made by the Crescent Negro Council to oppose the bond issue unless a positive statement on integration was included in the admission policies of the proposed Center. Adams, with help from McDonald, Hale, Simmons, and Erickson, played a decisive role, but while they set the pace, they at no time ignored the sub-community's organization which gave their power roles legitimacy.

Another issue affording a good opportunity to observe the Negro community in action is the selection of candidates for City Council who would receive the organized support of the Crescent sub-community. White candidates for councilmen-at-large or mayor (two-year terms) and, since 1948, a Negro candidate for City Council from the fifth, largely Negro ward (a four-year term) have been selected. I will consider primarily here the political campaigns of 1957 and 1959, though in order to understand what occurred in 1957 it is necessary to discuss first the campaigns of Nathan Banks, who was in 1953 elected the first Negro councilman in the history of Crescent City.

The Political Action Committee of the Crescent Negro Council selected Banks to run for City Council in 1949. He was defeated by the white candidate by 820 votes. In 1953 the Political Action Committee—including Bob Healy, R. E. Laroux, Sr., Alice Bradock, Ellwood Smith, O. G. Sherwood—again nominated Banks. This time he defeated his white opponent by 1000 votes. Banks had the support of the leaders of all Negro organizations. He was one of the sub-community's economic dominants and took an active part in community life. He had participated in the Crescent Negro Council since its inception in the 1930's and had held every major office in the Council. He was considered an effective representative of the Negro community.

John Miller had also been eager to run for the Council. He had been a member of the Political Action Committee and worked with the Democratic Party on the county and state levels. He was also chairman of the important Mid-South State Teachers Commission, a Negro education lobby. But Miller failed to get the approval of the power leaders because he too often insisted on going his own way, refusing the advice of the more powerful.

Banks soon proved his ability and became one of the most active members of the City Council, winning the admiration of the moderate and liberal white leaders. Following the announcement of the Supreme Court decision in 1954, the press asked Banks for a statement. Banks made his statement without discussing it with other minority leaders. He said he felt the court ruling should be upheld, but believed that time was needed for its implementation. He further suggested that, even if desegregation of schools were to come immediately to Crescent City, few Negro children would go to white schools. Most would continue to attend Negro schools near their homes with their friends.

Following the appearance of these remarks in the local paper, Howard Adams paid a visit to Banks's office. He advised Banks that his statement was unwise, even if true. It could be interpreted as evidence of a willingness to compromise and an expectation that things would remain much as they were. Others also indicated their displeasure. Certain Negro leaders believed that, though Banks was sincere in his efforts to perform his duties as a truly biracial leader and was not necessarily accommodative, he was simply not aggressive enough to face the changes wrought by the Supreme Court decision. Those who did feel that Banks was too eager to compromise found their suspicions confirmed as white leaders turned to him as spokesman of the sub-community instead of to other power leaders.

The first test of Banks's influence after his statement to the press came in the spring of 1955, when he asked the Political Action Committee to support George Carson as a white candidate for City Council. Carson and Banks had worked together on the City Council, and Banks felt that Carson was increasingly sympathetic to Negro needs. The committee was to make its recommendations to the Cres-

cent Negro Council early in May. Steven McDonald,
president of Negro Council, and Howard Adams were
present when the Committee—O. G. Sherwood, Charles
Driver, William Hoover, John Miller, and Stanley Lewis—
met, and a "tentative" slate was drawn up for presentation
to the Negro Council as a whole. It did not include Carson's name, and it passed without any major opposition
from the Council floor. From this time forward, according to Banks, he was unable to get a single motion
passed in the Negro Council. And when the Education
Committee drew up a petition urging the school board to
take immediate steps toward school desegregation, Nathan
Banks was not asked to sign it.

At no time was Banks informed that the support of the
Negro Council was being withdrawn, but that was what
was happening. During this period, nevertheless, both the
Negro and the white press continued to be favorably disposed toward Banks. Healy continued to point out that
Banks always gave consideration to the needs of his race.
The white press suggested that he was one of the more
conscientious councilmen, one who tried to be fair to both
racial groups.

In 1957 Banks, feeling that he could not run for re-
election without support from Adams or McDonald, announced that he would not seek a second term. His term
of office had served a very useful purpose, for Banks, by
proving that Negro leadership was capable and diplomatic,
had paved the way for a more aggressive member of the
sub-community to be elected to the City Council. The
power leaders selected McDonald to succeed Banks. Again
John Miller opposed the Political Action Committee candidate, but without success. On June 15, 1957, Steven
McDonald became the second successful Negro candidate
for City Council.

The election campaign of 1957 was one of the bitterest

in years. The incumbent candidate for mayor, Bert Murphy, was opposed by Donald Boyd. Boyd was a member of the Cranston family and president of Allied Container Corporation. He was backed by the conservative white leaders, who waged an anti-Negro campaign. Murphy, however, along with councilman-at-large candidates George Ronald, professor of economics at Southern University, and Sebert Tompkins and Vale Cort, two moderate whites, received Negro support and were elected.

The 1959 Council election campaign was a quiet one. The conservative element in the white community made little organized effort to achieve its ends, and Murphy was unopposed. O. G. Sherwood and Ellwood Smith became co-chairmen of the Political Action Committee, to replace chairman Healy, when Adams took over as president in the fall of 1957. This Committee, with David Hale, McDonald, and Adams attending, met in advance of the full Negro Council meeting of May 14, 1959, at which time white candidates for City Council might speak to the Negro group. By the time the candidates appeared, the Political Action Committee had already made its selection of a slate of approved candidates and had visited various white leaders in an effort to gauge their tempers and to extract certain promises in return for Negro community support.

The early part of the Crescent Negro Council meeting on May 14 was turned over to the Political Action Committee. Sherwood introduced the candidates. Jason Hartwig, representing labor, urged the Negroes to back him in order to revive the Negro-white labor voting block in the community. Three other men, including Donald Boyd and a Jewish candidate, Price Goldman, also spoke briefly. When these candidates had spoken and left, Sherwood presented the Political Action Committee report on the slate. Signed by Sherwood, Smith, Halan Barton, Parsons, Hale, McDonald, and Adams, the report "respectfully sug-

gested that the Council should back the candidacy of
Mayor Murphy, George Ronald, Donald Boyd, and Sebert
Tompkins."

The report met considerable opposition from the floor.
Stanley Lewis, Gus Harvey, and Rutherford Fortune—all
active on the Negro Labor Board—asked to be heard.
Lewis and Harvey felt that the Committee should recommend the labor leader, Jason Hartwig, on the strength of
his support of the rights and interests of Negro labor.
Fortune, however, saw Hartwig's concern for Negro labor
as an expedient gesture designed to obtain Negro political
support.   Fred Nelson, of Consolidated Insurance and
Realty, questioned the advisability of supporting Donald
Boyd because of Boyd's previous alignment with the reac-
tionaries and particularly his part in the 1957 anti-Negro
campaign.

At this point, Tom Marshall and Conrad May tried to
introduce on the floor a motion accepting the Political Action Committee report.   They and four other Council members had been briefed on the slate before the meeting in
order to insure the Committee of support from the floor—
a maneuver commonly used by the committee in past years.
But Fred Nelson, Charles Wareman, Art Troop, John Miller, Thurston Polk, Jim Oldes, Bob Healy, with others, demanded to be heard.   The Committee's efforts to control
debate collapsed.

The opposition was answered by Sherwood, Smith, Mc-
Donald, and Adams.   Each, in effect, said the Committee
had been very careful to choose those men who could do
the most for the Negro community and asked that Negro
Council members put their small personal preferences
aside and vote for the slate in order to present a united
front.   There was still opposition from the floor. At length,
Adams explained in detail the Committee's reasons for
supporting each individual.   He pointed out that the labor

leader and the Jewish candidate had little effective backing from the community groups and would be fairly ineffectual even if elected.

The opposition to Boyd was more difficult to silence, but Adams did it eloquently. He revealed that Boyd had come to his office following the 1957 campaign, ashamed and apologetic. Boyd confessed that he had been used by the conservative elements of Crescent City, including certain members of his family. Boyd gave Adams his promise to work constructively for Negro-white relations in the future and to give more support to Negro requests in the City Council.[1]

Following Adams' discussion, Erickson moved for a vote on the committee report. The Council voted to support the candidates recommended by the Political Action Committee. R. E. Laroux, Sr., spoke in praise of the Committee's efforts. Fred Nelson and Dick Laroux, Jr., were appointed to collect funds to help defray the cost of promoting the ticket. Lewis and Harvey were in charge of contacting labor to get out the vote, and Parsons, representing the Ministerial Council, was to urge ministers to make announcements encouraging the citizens to vote. The precinct committeemen would be contacted by Ellwood Smith and Alice Bradock. Campaign headquarters would, it was agreed, be located in one of Bob Healy's front offices. Trice Spock announced the slate of approved candidates at the Business League luncheon the Monday after the Negro Council meeting. Filtering through the various channels of the sub-community, the recommendations of the Negro Council were transmitted to the citizens, and on June 3, 1959, the Negro ticket was again victorious.

Thus far the power leaders had been able to make

1. That there had been a change of heart was apparent from my interview with Boyd. It seemed genuine. Adams, a perceptive individual who was inclined to be suspicious of such changes, was convinced of Boyd's sincerity.

substantial gains by means of political bargaining. While they have not always been as successful as they were in 1957 and 1959, there are indications that the effectiveness of political bargaining will increase in the next decade. Negro leaders will probably have to include broader sub-community representation in their policy-making. Their wise decisions in the past have served to solidify Negro political opinion, but sub-community members now show an inclination to disapprove of pre-selected slates. A greater degree of political participation is therefore to be expected in the future.

After 1954, a major area of concern to Negro leaders was the impending crisis over integration of Crescent City's public schools. Three other issues were closely related— efforts to establish a Mayor's Commission on Race Relations; the use of double sessions in certain of the Negro Schools, with subsequent proposals to turn over a condemned white school to Negro children; and a proposal for filing mass pupil reassignment applications. The interrelation of all these issues prompted me to treat them here simultaneously and in some detail.

The minority leaders made no move toward school integration until the Supreme Court's second, more explicit decree of May 31, 1955. Immediately after publication of that decree, the Education Committee of the Crescent Negro Council, chaired by Howard Adams, recommended that a statement from the Negro community be presented to the school board. Working with Adams in drawing up the petition were Charles Driver of Commercial Bank and Trust, William Hoover, Charles Wareman, and Jack Simmons. The petition, carrying 700 signatures of sub-community residents, was read to the Board of Education in June, 1955. The petitioners asked that the two racial groups meet to work out a program of compliance with the decisions of the Court. The school board thanked Adams and the other representatives, but would say no more. The Negro group left the meeting baffled by the unexpected lack of communication.

In the meantime, the state legislature was working on the first of a series of measures designed to circumvent the Court's ruling. The Pupil Assignment Bill was before the House when a group of Negro leaders throughout the state joined together to oppose it. Bob Healy was chairman of this group, which called itself the Committee of 100. The Committee selected Steven McDonald to speak for the Negroes before the legislature. Despite his pleas, the bill was enacted late in 1955. It created a system for assigning specific students to specific schools on "grounds other than race." Other law passed at that time included a so-called local-option plan for suspending operation of public schools by a majority vote in any school district.

In the fall and winter of 1956 to 1957, Crescent City Negro leaders launched a campaign to obtain the admittance of Negro children to white schools within the framework of the state laws. In order to protect the attorneys active on behalf of the Crescent Negro Council and the local chapter of the N.A.A.C.P. from the barratry laws of the state, a special committee made up of representatives from the Negro associations was formed to provide assistance to parents in understanding the provisions of the law. Power-of-attorney forms were made available by the committee to parents who wished to petition the school board. Key members of this special committee included William Hoover, Dr. Charles Wareman, Charles Driver, Reverend D. E. Jackson, Jack Simmons, Orville Robbins, and Tom Piper, a young executive at Southern Life Insurance. Steven McDonald was official chairman. Sixty-five parents signed power-of-attorney forms naming O. G. Sherwood, Harris Erickson, Conrad May, Tom Marshall, and Howard Adams as attorneys to represent them in obtaining reassignment of their children to all-white schools.

Of this group of sixty-five, fourteen sent letters to the school board in July, 1957, seeking assignment of their children to white schools beginning in the 1957 to 1958 academic year. The board delayed its preliminary notices of assignment until August 14, 1957. No Negro youngsters were assigned to white schools. The parents of nine pupils then filed formal application for reassignment of their children to white schools. These applications were rejected in September and again in October. The lawyers acting on behalf of the parents had then exhausted all remedies available under the Mid-South State Pupil Assignment Law.

The next step was to file suit with the Circuit Court, something the Negro leaders had wanted to avoid because of the delay and expense that would result. They had hoped that the white leaders of Crescent City would voluntarily comply with the Supreme Court ruling, following the example of three neighboring cities. But the members of the school board, especially Fulton, its chairman, had decided that school desegration would be more acceptable to the white community if it came about through litigation. Many, though not all, of the white leaders agreed with Fulton's position. Because the few who did not agree were unable to influence the white community at large, it reacted to the issue with obstructionism and delay, though not with actual formal resistance.

There occurred at this time, however, a stirring at the grass roots of community leadership. A few individuals in both the white and Negro sub-communities, alarmed by the lack of communication on school desegregation, felt that contact and exchange should be encouraged. Mrs. Stratton Springer and Oscar Ford, both secondary power leaders in the white structure, had independently been thinking of ways to bring the two races together. Dr. Charles Wareman, Nathan Banks, and Silas Alder of the Negro community had also been wondering what might be done.

Late in August, 1957, Mrs. Springer called a small biracial group together at her home to discuss race relations in Crescent City. At this first meeting Wareman, Banks, Alder, and Adams represented the Negro community. From the white community Mrs. Springer was able to get two faculty members of Southern University, one physician and his wife, and the editor of one of the local newspapers to attend. Little was accomplished at this initial gathering, but the group decided to talk to others and to meet again in the fall.

On October 1, 1957, a second meeting was held at the home of Mr. and Mrs. Springer. Of the original group, the editor and Howard Adams were missing, but Ford was in attendance. Plans were laid for a larger meeting the following week at Ford's home. Ford persuaded three of his more influential friends to attend, including Potter Worth, president of the Crescent City Real Estate Company. Others from the two white colleges attended, along with Mrs. Springer, Wareman, Alder, and Banks. It was at this gathering that the decision was made to circulate a petition among Crescent City leaders of both races requesting the Mayor to appoint a Commission on Race Relations.

The first petition was drawn up the following week, and on October 10, 1957, Mrs. Springer visited Jack Vale III, seeking his assistance. Vale was not enthusiastic. He felt that the proposed organization would have little authority and therefore little effect. But he was willing to help. He pointed out weaknesses in the draft and advised Mrs. Springer to rewrite it. He also consented to work with the committee and offered the committee the use of his office.

The revised petition was circulated during the last two weeks in October. Both conservative and moderate white leaders signed. Signatories from the white community included Roger Cranston, president of the Bulletin Publishing Company; Jack Vale III; Richard Bosworth, president of Piedmont National Bank; Vale Cort, Jr., and Potter Worth of the Crescent City Real Estate Company; Farsworth Pennman, president of the Mid-South Life Insurance Company and Chamber of Commerce president; Dr. Andrew Hadley, president of Southern University; and a number of top representatives of labor, medicine, law and religion. In the Negro community Nathan Banks, Silas Alder, and I. N. Karns, among others, added their names.

On November 4, 1957, the petition requesting the establishment of a Commission on Race Relations was submitted to Mayor Bert Murphy. The following night, the Mayor presented it to the City Council, indicating that he favored such an organization. The petition received additional backing on the City Council from George Ronald, Sebert Tompkins, and Fred Bardox, a white power figure and owner of one of the largest commercial firms in the city. The Council gave its approval, establishing a three-man committee headed by Bert Murphy to select the nine members of the Mayor's Commission on Race Relations. It was not until January of the following year that the City Council was able to fill the last of the nine seats on the Commission on Race Relations. Appointments included representatives of both the conservative and liberal elements of the city. Early in January the newspapers announced that Roger Cranston, Oscar Ford, Silas Alder, Dr. Albert French, Nathan Banks, and others had agreed to serve. The Commission's formal purpose was to sponsor programs designed to increase good will and reduce tension, to assist each race to understand the position of the other in order that they might meet and solve current problems, and to serve as a public forum in which the views of all groups might be sought and expressed without fear of recrimination.

But there were still pitfalls ahead for the Commission, and the first blow came from where it was least expected— the Negro community. What seemed to be a basic disagreement occurred between the Negro leaders directly involved in the school integration struggle and other Negro leaders. Banks, Karns, and Alder felt the Race Relations Commission represented a possible breakthrough in the area of communications in the city. Here was a way that integration might be settled peaceably and out of court. For other leaders, however, the Commission was a faltering and tardy effort that actually might become a stumbling block in the way of desegregation.

From the first, Adams and McDonald had been lukewarm to the idea of a race relations commission. After the first meeting Adams excused himself from other sessions because of "pressure of business and other responsibilities." The two men did not feel that a powerless organ of the sort could be of value in the desegregation battle. Too, plans were already under way for the next step in the sub-community's fight for desegregated schools. The younger leaders were afraid that an attempt to work through the Commission on Race Relations might delay these plans. O. G. Sherwood, in fact, stopped by Silas Alder's office before the first meeting of the Commission on January 20, 1958, to remind Alder that the N.A.A.C.P. lawyers planned to bring suit against the Crescent City school board and the State Board of Education on January 31, 1958, *unless* the Race Relations Commission could arrange for a meeting very soon between the Negro leaders and the

City school board.   Sherwood asked Alder to pass this information on to the Commission.

This move was interpreted by some members of the Commission, including Banks and Ford, as an attempt on the part of the Negro leadership to scuttle the Race Relations Commission.   But the Negro leaders insisted they had been on the point of acting and were now willing to detour to give the Commission a chance before continuing their plans for litigation.   There was undoubtedly some truth in both interpretations.

While Alder had known that a desegregation suit was planned, he was not aware of the details.   He reported on his meeting with Sherwood at the first meeting of the Commission.   The "ultimatum" from the Negro leadership meant that the Commission would have to deal with the desegregation issue without having had an opportunity to lay any of the necessary groundwork.   Nevertheless, the members agreed to do what they could and asked for a meeting with other Negro leaders.

On January 21, 1958, Alder called Sherwood and relayed the Commission's request for a meeting with some of the Negro leaders.   Sherwood contacted Howard Adams and William Hoover.   They decided that a small committee should be formed representing the N.A.A.C.P. and the Crescent Negro Council.   On the evening of January 24, the Reverend D. E. Jackson, Sherwood, Hoover, Erickson, Conrad May, and Adams got together to make plans for their meeting with the Commission on Race Relations.   The following week this group, with Hoover serving as spokesman, consulted with the Commission and advised it that Negro leaders wanted to sit down with the school board to help to work out a plan of desegregation.   No mention was made at this meeting of an impending lawsuit against the school board.   The Commission on Race Relations promised to meet with the school board as soon as possible, and the board agreed to place the Commission's report on its March, 1958, agenda. The power leaders of the sub-community, still hoping to avoid a suit, decided to defer litigation until after the March meeting.

While the Commission and the Negro spokesmen awaited the outcome of that meeting, three resignations were submitted to the City Council by members of the Commission. On March 3, 1958, the City Council voted unanimously for the appointment of Nathan Banks to the school board, and to avoid a "conflict of interest," Banks resigned from the Commission. The appointment of Banks to the board was a real victory for the Negro leaders. They had been trying for several years to persuade the City Council to appoint a Negro school board member. Finally, by throwing their support to City Council candidates who had agreed to nominate a Negro to the school board and by refraining from asking Council members for a committment to a specific Negro candidate for the appointment, they were successful. The victory came at a most strategic time.

Other resignations from the Commission came from Roger Cranston and Harold Peters. Cranston, a conservative white leader, was not willing to be associated with the Commission's efforts to bring the Negro leadership and the city school board to an agreement on school desegregation. He gave as his reason for resigning "heavy business responsibilities." Peters, another conservative, soon followed Cranston's lead. It was a very wobbly six-member Commission that appeared before the school board on the evening of March 15, 1958.

Oscar Ford addressed the board the evening of the much-awaited meeting. After preliminary remarks, he said, "This is our purpose in being here—members of the Negro community want to sit down and talk with you in an informal manner." His remarks were greeted by silence.

No questions were asked; no comments were made. When Ford asked what interpretation could be placed on the silence, the chairman replied, "Interpret it simply as silence." And with that the Commission's appearance before the Board of Education was at an end. Ironically, the next item of business on the school board agenda was the administration of the oath to its first Negro member, Nathan Banks.

Alder notified Adams of the results. Ford relayed the Board's "silence is silence" reaction to William Hoover in an official letter. On March 17, 1958, Ford was present at the City Council meeting to report on the affair. He told the Council that the Commission would not forsake the task of keeping lines of communication open. The Council appointed a new three-man committee headed by Mayor Murphy to nominate the successors to the Commission members who had resigned. It was not until October, 1958, that the City Council was able to fill the vacancies. To do so they had to ignore the recommendation of the Crescent Negro Council executive committee that either Hoover or Parsons be appointed to fill Banks's place, for the white leaders selected by the City Council would not accept their appointments unless the remaining appointment was also given to a white. It was not until late in the following year that the biracial Commission began to achieve any of its purposes, as we shall see later. In the meantime, both Negroes and whites felt that the Commission was all but dead.

With predictions about the ineffectiveness of the Race Relations Commission apparently now confirmed, Sherwood proceeded with the school desegregation suit. On May 18, 1958, suit was filed by two Negro mothers on behalf of their sons. One of the plaintiffs was William Hoover's wife. The long process of litigation had begun. Not in the forefront of the battle but known to be working to obtain financial support for the suits were several of the economic dominants. The sub-community leadership rallied around those who had carried the brunt of the burden, and the ranks of the Negro community were once more closed.

Pre-trial hearings with a federal judge were held in August and again in September and December of 1958, with Sherwood acting as chief counsel for the two plaintiffs. Erickson, May, and Adams assisted him. Delays followed so that questions might be raised and answered on both sides. The date for the trial was moved from January to March, 1959.

In the interim there arose another issue pertaining to public education, and the minority leaders again went into action. On August 26, 1958, the city school board notified parents of children attending one of the elementary schools in the northern end of town that lack of schoolroom space necessitated double sessions. The parents became concerned and contacted the Education Committee of the Crescent Negro Council for assistance. Jack Simmons and his Committee began work on a petition against the move. It was signed by interested persons and presented by Simmons on September 7, 1958, before the school board. The petition listed several reasons why double sessions were detrimental to the children and parents involved. It ended by stating that the overcrowded conditions of the school involved could be overcome simply by transferring some of the Negro children to nearby white schools. The board agreed to seek more buses in which to transport the Negro children to less crowded Negro schools, but they would not discuss the transfer of Negro youngsters to white schools.

In September ten requests for reassignment to white schools were filed by Negro parents on behalf of their children. The requests were turned down. In October six

parents asked that the board reconsider its September decision. When the board met, Nathan Banks moved that
the parents be allowed to defer their requests for reassignment until the impending litigation in respect to integration
of Crescent City schools was settled. The other members
of the school board would not second this motion, since it
implied that it would be only a matter of time until reassignment requests might be approved. It was therefore
struck from the minutes.

In March, 1959, the city school superintendent and
the school business manager suggested that overcrowding
in the North-End Negro schools could be alleviated by
turning over to Negroes the Boulevard School, a white
school which had been abandoned in 1957. The Negro
school administrators in North-End notified the North-End
P.T.A. of this intention, and it, in turn, notified the sub-
community P.T.A. Council. Charles Driver, president of
this latter group, sent a memorandum to the Crescent Negro
Council about the proposal to use the condemned school,
and Adams forwarded the memorandum to Simmons of the
Education Committee, advising him to get in touch with
the superintendent of schools to arrange an inspection of
the old Boulevard School. Simmons, Driver, John Bronton, Peter Martin, Jr., and a member of the department of
architecture at Mid-South College met with the School
Superintendent later that month for an inspection of the
school.

The Education Committee made an unfavorable report
of its inspection to the Crescent Negro Council the following week. The Council, as a result, gave it authorization
to draw up a petition of protest to be presented to the
Crescent school board. Simmons, Driver, Bronton, and
Martin wrote the first draft, which was then revised and ap-
praised from the legal point of view by Adams, Sherwood,
and Erickson. The petition was reviewed and signed by

several Negro P.T.A. units, by the president of the Negro P.T.A. Council, by the local chapter of the N.A.A.C.P., and by the Crescent Negro Council.

The city superintendent of schools agreed to put the Negro request for a hearing on the April school board agenda. Over seventy Negroes attended the meeting as Simmons presented the protest against the reopening of an "abandoned and structurally inferior building, and more particularly against the creation of a new Jim-Crow public school." The protest cited eight major defects in the building. Simmons ended by pointing out that the board could easily solve the overcrowding of segregated Negro schools simply by desegregating the schools.

Perhaps the most significant aspect of this meeting was that for the first time the white members of the board were communicative. Fulton had opened the session by declaring that it would be concerned with three items only—the Boulevard School, double sessions, and transportation—but the Negro leaders maneuvered him into saying "We aren't ready for integration." From this point on, the Negroes present discussed integration at some length.

The school board met again in May and reviewed the Negro protest concerning the old Boulevard School. The position of the board was shaky, and it decided upon a significant maneuver. It voted to invite a number of the ex-officio leaders from Negro business, clergy, and education circles to meet with it and discuss further the possibility of opening the old Boulevard School—people not directly concerned with the original protest. The list included Dr. French, Dr. Ruth Johnson, Dean Osgood Hendrix of the Mid-South College Graduate School, I. N. Karns, Reverend Jackson, Bob Healy, and John Barton. Peter Martin, Jr., and Jack Simmons of the original group were also included at the insistence of Banks. The invitation was issued on May 5 for the evening of May 7.

Simmons met Adams and McDonald at the Wednesday Luncheon Club and informed them of the school board's latest move. It was decided that the invited group should get together the next day to review the whole case. Simmons contacted the group by phone, and a meeting was arranged in Dr. French's office the afternoon of May 6. Simmons reviewed the entire file on the Boulevard School issue for those present. The group agreed that under no conditions would it support the reopening of the building.

Fulton indicated at the outset of the conference on May 7 that discussion of integration was not in order. The Negro leaders disregarded his ruling. Each of them stated that he was opposed to the reopening of the Boulevard School and that the Board must think in terms of integration as the solution. Bob Healy's statement was typical. "Not one of us," said Healy, "would go back to our people and recommend the use of that old building. We would be repudiated and scorned if we did. Integration is the answer to crowded Negro schools, and it's time action was taken."

The newspapers carried a full account of this school board meeting (the first such account since Nathan Banks had been appointed) and the ensuing discussion of school desegregation. The channels of communication were opened and the sub-community's push for a shift in policies was beginning to make itself felt. The white members of the Board had not been prepared for the solidarity of the Negroes—especially of those Negroes they had especially selected themselves. They had deferred action on the Boulevard School issue at their regular May meeting, and they did so again at the June meeting. Finally the plan was entirely dropped, and in January, 1960, it was announced that the Boulevard School property was to be auctioned off, with funds from its sale going to the construction of a new wing on one of the Negro elementary schools.

Oral arguments in the Crescent City integration suit, meanwhile, had begun in the Middle District Court in March, 1959. Originally filed to test the constitutionality of the Pupil Assignment Law and the local-option plan, the suit had by this time concentrated on the question of whether or not the plaintiffs had been denied reassignment on the basis of race, after having duly exhausted all administrative remedies provided by the state. Hearings were concluded on April 1, 1959. Final papers and briefs were scheduled for filing with the judge in the following two months. The State Board of Education and the city school board moved for dismissal of the suit. Their motion was deferred.

At the April 9, 1959, meeting of the Crescent Negro Council, Erickson and May, as co-chairmen of the Legal Redress Committee, reported on the status of the suit. O. G. Sherwood also made some comments—one of them of particular significance and an anticipation of things to come. He said that, since the Supreme Court had already ruled segregation illegal, it seemed foolish to him to bring just one or two cases before the courts. Rather, a suit might have a better chance for success if filed by a large number of applicants for reassignment.

Between April 9 and April 14, 1959, a small group of men—McDonald, Hoover, Sherwood, Adams, Erickson, Healy, and Wareman—got together to map out the new strategy for breaking the segregated pattern of the schools. The new policy centered about mass reassignment applications to the city school board. There was some indication that the court might decide that the plaintiffs had not exhausted all administrative remedies in seeking admission to white schools. It might, in this event, simply continue the case. Even if the suit were decided in favor of the plaintiffs, only one or two admissions would result, at best. The Negro leaders agreed that the mass reassignment application plan should go into effect, whether or not the court case was won.

The Education Committee was alerted to the new plan for obtaining a large number of applicants for reassignment. Dr. Peter Ware, surgeon at Washington Hospital and a member of the Education Committee, urged the committee to begin a series of mass meetings in the various churches to encourage parents to apply for reassignment of their children. Simmons, however, advised the Committee that it should wait until it heard from the Crescent Negro Council Executive Committee or some of the other leaders.

On the afternoon of April 14, while I myself was meeting with Simmons in his office, a call came from William Hoover. Hoover informed Simmons that a decision had been reached regarding the mass reassignment plan. The first of a series of mass meetings to reach the sub-community masses would be held April 26 at the St. John's African Methodist Episcopal Church.

Following this April 26 meeting, Charles Wareman appeared before the Ministerial Council to request that the fourth Sunday in May be set aside in each church to permit various sub-community leaders to urge parents to petition for reassignment of their children. At the May 14 meeting of the Crescent Negro Council, Wareman reported that the Ministerial Council had agreed. In the meantime, Charles Driver, working with the Negro P.T.A. Council, was informing all parents affiliated with the Negro P.T.A.'s throughout the city of the plan. The power leaders clearly were taking a vigorous stand. They were tired of silence and delay. They had determined to find ways to strengthen their bargaining power in the biracial community.

There was another indication that the strategy of the top policy-makers of the sub-community was shifting. Howard Adams met Jack Vale and Bill Stratton of the white community on April 17 to discuss an economic program the latter two wished to have approved by the state legislature. Following this conference Adams and Vale remained for an "off-the-record" talk in Adams' office. In the course of their three-hour discussion, Adams hinted at the new policies the minority community was going to employ until desegregation in major areas of the community had been achieved. Some of the Negro leaders had decided that the Negro community had done all it could do for the moment. Now it was time to force the hands of the more liberal and progressive white leaders of the city. Instead of backing progressive community projects, which had been a Negro policy for the past 25 years, it would be necessary to withdraw support from these projects until Negroes were given their rightful voice in community life. Since the white leadership was aware that constructive growth in Crescent City was often dependent upon the Negro vote, it would have to choose between the safety of silence on the race question and the possibility of seeing the development of the community come to a halt. Negroes realized this tack was a gamble that might not work at the current stage of Crescent race relations, but they were willing to try it.

Through the early summer months of 1959, the mass reassignment plans moved quietly forward. On July 20 the city school board again asked for the dismissal of the school desegregation case in the federal court on the basis that the plantiffs had not exhausted all admission remedies. Again the motion for dismissal was deferred.

On August 5, 1959, the city school board announced that it would follow its traditional pupil-assignment policies for the 1959 to 1960 school year. At that board meeting Banks made a very strong plea for integration. "After five years of waiting, steps must be taken in compliance with the Supreme Court's decision," said Banks. He moved that the School Board amend its policy for the coming year and make reassignment without regard to race. His motion received no second.

The following day Jack Simmons released a statement to the press saying that there would be "several" new applications for reassignment. Negro parents had the ten days following August 21, 1959, in which to make their applications. By August 24 approximately one hundred parents had filed application for reassignment of their children to white schools. The evening papers carried the story with banner headlines and described the mass application as the first broadside attack on segregation in Crescent City's schools. The school board (with the exception, of course, of Banks) and most of the rest of the white community were taken by surprise. By August 25 the number of applications had risen to 225, and Fulton called the school board into executive session.

On August 26 the Board announced that it had denied reassignment to 201 of the applicants, but would continue to deliberate on the requests of the remaining 24. Sherwood, chairman of the state and local N.A.A.C.P. Legal Redress Committee, and Kevin Botony, state president of the N.A.A.C.P. from nearby Brownsville, were bombarded with questions about the N.A.A.C.P.'s part in leading this mass movement.[2] Sherwood and Botony deflected all such questions by observing that they did not solicit requests of assistance but only supplied aid when asked. Sherwood, Erickson, Adams, May, and Marshall served as legal advisers to the parents involved in the mass reassignment plan.

2. A notion common among many of the leaders and citizens of Crescent City's white population is that the N.A.A.C.P. controls the Crescent Negro Council. However, as is evident throughout this study, the N.A.A.C.P. has a supplementary and often secondary role to that of the broader and much more powerful Crescent Negro Council. The leadership structures interlock, but it was through the Crescent Negro Council that the mass reassignment program was developed and came to fruition.

The Crescent City papers began predicting that there would be "mixing in the schools"—the Negro paper called it "token integration." On August 29, 1959, the city school board announced that it had admitted eight Negro children to four white schools. Fulton in his press release said that the Board had acted after "five years of careful study." Negro and many white leaders were amused by the reference to "careful study," but the white population at large seemed to be placated, and that was Fulton's aim. The school board had avoided action for as long as it dared. The Negro leaders would not be stopped, and several of the white leaders had advised Fulton that it was time to act.

Nathan Banks asked that the school board approve integration in principle. His motion received no second. Mayor Murphy called for "calmness, courtesy, and acceptance of integration as an inevitability of the laws of the land." He mentioned the high caliber of Negro and white leadership in Crescent City that would be an important factor in making integration in Crescent City a successful endeavor. The city superintendent of schools also supported the school board decision and asked white teachers and citizens to accept it. There was no violence, there were no demonstrations.

On September 5 the Crescent Court handed down his ruling on *Hoover and Catton vs. the Crescent City Board of Education.* He ruled against the Negro plaintiffs because they had not exhausted the possibilities of relief offered in state statutes regarding assignment of pupils. "Another conclusion might easily have been reached had the plaintiffs performed the simple duties imposed on them by state law," said Judge Saunders. He gave the plaintiffs ten days to avail themselves of a continuance by first exhausting their recourses under the assignment laws. "For," said the judge, "the Crescent City school board is to be criticized. The pattern of their assignment notices and their delay in making assignments in past years suggest that their reassignments have been made or denied solely on the basis of race or color."

One of Hoover's sons had been admitted to a white school in the mass reassignment move, the other had not. Negro attorneys asked for a continuation of the lawsuit so that he might exhaust all remedies of the state's admission procedures. Hoover appeared before the school board on September 12, with Howard Adams serving as his spokesman. If the board denied the Hoover boy's petition, his case would return to the court, where it was almost certain to be treated favorably. The board therefore admitted the second Hoover boy to a previously all-white high school on September, 18, 1959—two years after he first applied.

Of the 201 reassignment applications denied, 165 were submitted for reconsideration. Hearings on these appeals were held on September 19, and they were again rejected. But the door was now open for mass litigation, should the Negro leaders decide to expand the limited integration they had won.[3] The top Negro leaders had won a round in their fight for equality and power in Crescent City.

During his first year and a half as a school board member, Banks had used the diplomatic approach which had been so effective when he was a member of the City Council. By 1959, however, he realized that a truly partisan approach was necessary. Following the new strategy of the other leaders, he announced late in 1959 that he would not support the proposed six-million-dollar bond issue for new city schools "if it continues segregation in the schools." "I am unalterably opposed to the bond issue if it facilitates segregation," stated Banks, "despite the fact that I recognize the need for its passage in order to provide nec-

3. In spring, 1960, suits were filed for 161 children denied admittance in 1959. The Crescent Negro Council also laid plans to obtain desegregation in county schools.

essary classroom space for the prospective school populations." Only if the school board were to adopt a basic geographical admission policy and a liberal reassignment program permitting transfer of qualified students to schools where courses of study more appropriate to their interests and abilities were offered would Banks recommend and support the issue. The new policy began to take shape, and the leaders of the sub-community were once more united in their efforts to make it effective. For many of the older leaders, it was too late to learn the habit of speaking and acting forcefully, but the younger men, whose courage and ambition led them to take such stands, found their positions of power in the Negro community strengthened.

Since 1955 there have been a number of attempts to break segregated patterns in other areas of city life. In 1956 the Civic Committee of the Negro Council—including Charles Driver, chairman, and Richard Laroux, Sr., Professor Joseph Goode, and Stanley Lewis—obtained permission from the local government to use the tennis courts in Woodland Park, to which Negroes had not previously been admitted, for a series of Negro tournaments. Subsequently some of the Negro citizens attempted to use the courts for private play and were ejected. Banks, Adams, Karns, McDonald, and Driver conferred with the mayor, the city manager, and the police chief. A compromise was reached by the terms of which Negroes would make no mass moves to utilize white recreation facilities and white officials would no longer eject or prosecute individual Negroes seeking the use of such facilities. (The swimming pools were not, and have not as yet become, an issue.) Other meetings between Negro and white leaders followed, and quiet agreement was reached to desegregate the city buses, the ball park, and the Urban Renewal Board.

Not all attempts to break segregated patterns have originated with the most powerful Negro leaders, however. One of the most interesting shifts in the Negro power structure has been the increasing involvement of some of the younger and more militant Negroes in protest activities. Art Troop is a case in point. He is a thirty-year-old educational director of a middle-class church and adviser to Mid-South College's Baptist students. For the past four or five years, Troop has carried on a one-man crusade, battling both white and Negro leaders of Crescent City. He has been described by his critics as "irresponsible, opportunistic, and dangerous."

In 1956 he demanded to be allowed to use the white public library, to be admitted to the largest Crescent City theater, and to be admitted to the graduate school of Southern University, a private institution. He made a protest appearance before the City Council in 1957 and was subsequently given a card to the library. McDonald took up the matter of the theater to see what might legally be done, since the building is city property. During the summer of 1957 Troop and a group of Mid-South College students demanded service at a white hamburger stand. They were arrested and convicted of trespassing. Troop then went to the N.A.A.C.P. and demanded and received counsel. The case lost in the local, superior, and state supreme courts before Sherwood could persuade Troop to drop it. The Crescent Negro Council gave Troop no formal support. The Ministerial Council, at the insistence of Kyser and Bradock, went on record as opposed to the suit.

In September, 1959, the students at Mid-South College began to complain about the separate white and Negro "Welcome-College-Students" days sponsored by the Crescent City Merchants Association. Troop heard of the dissatisfaction and was soon at the center of the protest, organizing a boycott. A petition charging prejudicial treatment was drafted and sent to the Merchants' Association. An orderly boycott and protest parade were planned. Troop called in two other militant young Negroes to assist him—the Reverend Orville Robbins and Thurston Polk. Though they went to Tom Marshall for legal advice, their protest received only informal support from the power leaders or organizations.

The Merchants' Association became concerned about the projected demonstrations and turned to the Commission on Race Relations for help. It was at this stage that the Commission began to regain some of its prestige. It met with student representatives and members of the Merchants' Association on several occasions. An agreement was finally reached under which the Merchants' Association would sponsor a "Welcome-College-Students" week each fall for all college students regardless of race, but it would no longer provide the free favors and food it formerly had. While Troop was not present at the actual meetings, he was always close by to "advise" the student leaders before and after each session.

Early in 1960 the Negro struggle against segregation shifted noticeably from the legal arena to the market place. There occurred a series of student passive-resistance demonstrations against segregated chain store lunch counters all over the South. The college students of Crescent City were soon involved. The morning the Mid-South College student leaders began their sit-down demonstrations, Art Troop and Thurston Polk were notified, as was Tom Marshall. Troop appeared at the store chosen as the site of the demonstrations. Soon Troop, with Polk as his assistant, had taken over as the "official leader and spokesman" of the group. Marshall remained in the background.

Some of the students resented Troop's interference, but enough others felt his assistance was necessary that, when they and student leaders from other cities met and organized a student action committee, Troop was selected as executive secretary. This committee, incidentally, was not the only such state-wide committee; a number of others professing to speak for the students sprang up in other areas of the state.

Troop contacted the Reverend Martin Luther King and arranged to have him speak at a meeting of Crescent students and interested sub-community citizens. Troop notified none of the officials of the Crescent Negro Council or of any other Negro organization. It remained for Marshall and Polk to serve as emissaries to other sub-community leaders. They informed Steven McDonald of the plans to bring King to the city. McDonald, Adams, Sherwood, Alder, Healy and others greeted King at the airport when he arrived and attended the meeting at which he spoke. But it was Troop's show and he let no one forget it.

In the first days of the student protest, Tom Marshall urged the leaders of the Crescent Negro Council to speak out in favor of the movement. On the fourth day, Howard Adams issued a statement to the press—one that he, McDonald, Marshall, and others on the executive committee had drafted. This statement expressed sympathy with the student group. It stated that the Council was neither officially nor unofficially notified of the protest, but that, since the students were conducting themselves in an orderly fashion, they were to be commended for their efforts to end unfair discrimination. A statement from the Ministerial Council soon followed that, at the urging of Robbins, Parsons, and Jackson, expressed sympathy with the student demonstration. The white Council of Churches also backed the student group, as did the Women's Student Government of Southern University. It was, of course the orderly student demonstrators that were being supported, but by such support Troop found his own position enhanced.

In the meantime, Mayor Murphy requested that President French ask the students to meet with the Commission on Race Relations in order to come to an agreement on lunch counter policies. French set up a faculty committee to work out the arrangements, and the faculty committee declared that the students must arbitrate. Some students, however, continued to demonstrate.

Troop continued to ignore the power structure of the sub-community, as well as the college administration. He issued daily reports to the press and called for a boycott of business establishments refusing food service to Negroes. There is no doubt that Troop was something of an opportunist. It is likely that he perceived in the passive-resistance movement a means of vindication for his court defeat in the so-called Watson Hamburger Shop Case. Furthermore, in fall, 1959, he had been accepted as a member of a foreign missionary group and planned to depart for service with it in June, 1960. He could obviously act without concern for ultimate consequences, even though the students he led would eventually have to turn to the stable leaders of the sub-community for legal counsel and financial assistance. At the time this study was in preparation for publication, while there had been no clear outcome to the student demonstrations, it was evident that the established Negro leadership in Crescent City was already providing such assistance.

In no sense do I claim that this study has considered the full range of issues that came before Negro decision-makers in Crescent City. The issues I have discussed are, however, representative of those that have faced the sub-community during the past three years. To an extent, they are also representative of the basic issues facing the biracial community as a whole. Equally, I have not discussed the roles of all the leaders associated with the issues, but I have bent every effort to picture the process of decision-making in Crescent City accurately and responsibly. Many projects besides those mentioned here were directed by the same power leaders, and this is some evidence, at least, that my re-creation is true and typical.

Many of the day-to-day decisions made in a given community may, of course, involve neither controversial issues nor a nucleus of power leaders.[4] One would expect decisions in the constant processes of organizational and institutional life to be made by functionaries who may or may not be representatives of community power leaders. But such decisions are concerned with the routine operation of sub-community organization, and as such cannot necessarily be considered as basic community issues.

Rossi and others have criticized research on decision-makers for concentrating on community controversies.[5] Actually, the term "issue" in its basic sense suggests a point of debate among groups at variance with one another. Some controversy is therefore implicit in any study of community issues. Especially is it true that issues evolving in a biracial community are more likely to be controversial than those evolving in other communities. Negro protest can be projected into a wide range of areas, and in Crescent City the Negro's ability to transform issues into full-blown controversies is an important source of power.

The investigation of issues and decisions has revealed a significant correspondence between the 31 persons selected as power nominees and the persons who actually played roles as active decision-makers, who were what I call "power leaders." Approximately 71 per cent of the top power and sub-power nominees were active in most

4. Peter H. Rossi, "Community Decision Making," *Administrative Science Quarterly*, 1 (March, 1957), 439.

5. *Ibid.*, pp. 440-41. See also Ernest A. T. Barth and S. D. Johnson, "Community Power and a Typology of Social Issues," *Social Forces*, 38 (October, 1959), 29.

issues.   Over half were active at decision- and policy-making levels on all issues considered.   Others tended to specialize in some areas.   Of course, slightly different combinations of leaders and complexes of interests tended to occur in specific issues or phases of issues.   It was nevertheless quite clear that Crescent City's Negro community does have a group of leaders that remains much the same from issue to issue, owing, perhaps, in part to the fact that as a minority group it has had less opportunity and time to develop specialists.

Of the 29 per cent of the power (4 of the 10) and sub-power (5 of the 21) nominees who were not active in most local issues, some were active in functional and cosmopolitan issues, some were key members of the sub-community institutional and class structure and were "leaders" by virtue of personal esteem or official prestige, and some had lately been considered too accommodative and had in consequence lost influence on the policy-making level.

Any attempt to develop a precise hierarchy of power among the leaders would be abortive.   Many leaders whose sociometric ranking placed them as sub-power nominees were found to have as much—and in some cases more—access to decision-making roles as did those six power leaders who were among the top ten power nominees.   And below these power leaders were a large number of lesser leaders who did not initiate sub-community policy and action but who were vital in implementing decisions once they were arrived at.   These lesser leaders had, through their participation in the more influential associations, rather direct access to sub-community power.

While my study of minority leadership in action disclosed a cohesive group of power leaders, it did, nevertheless, reveal some dissension in this group (and between them and other leaders).   Their common goal has been to present a united front to the white community, however, and the astute maneuvering and compromise that have taken place within the power structure have allowed Negro leaders to reach a consensus on basic community issues and to move with some degree of purpose toward predetermined goals. The Crescent Negro Council serves as the organizational framework through which consensus in major subcommunity decisions is achieved and the full resources of the minority community are applied in the interest of obtaining serious readjustments of Crescent City's power structure.

CHAPTER VI

INTERGROUP AND INTRAGROUP COMMUNICATION AND RESPONSE

THE decision-making process in Crescent City is not as closed as the process in some communities studied. Hunter stressed the tenuous lines of communication and interaction between the power figures and the community at large. He emphasized the lack of communication between Negro and white leaders, and thereby the lack of awareness the various leadership structures have of one another. While Hunter may be right about Regional City, in Crescent City the lines of communication are not so attenuated within the sub-community itself or between the sub-community and the community at large.

The preceding chapter indicates that decisions made by both white and Negro leaders are often determined in terms of the influence which other individuals or groups may have on them or in terms of the consequences of the decisions themselves. This implies some form of communication. The present chapter accordingly is concerned with indicating the lines of communication within the sub-community and between it and the white community and with illustrating, indirectly at least, how the attitudes and actions of the Negro leaders reflect an awareness of the attitudes of other segments of the community about the issue of desegregation.

Communal rather than individual interests are more often served by decisions reached on basic sub-community issues.   Leaders seldom make decisions which they feel to be unacceptable to the majority of sub-community members.   This situation lends a certain credence to two related suppositions regarding Negro leadership.   First, Negro leaders, as individuals, are functionally related to and implicated in a system of mutual expectations, established and maintained in group interaction.   Second, the further the minority community leader departs from the expectations of his articulate followers, the greater the chance that he will prove unsuccessful as a leader.[1]

Leaders and informants in the sub-community were asked to list the organizations that were most influential in shaping the policies of the Negro community.   Some 97.5 per cent of the Negro leaders and 93.7 per cent of the sub-community members voted for the same ten organizations, although not in the same order: the Crescent Negro Council, the Negro Business League, the N.A.A.C.P., the Ministerial Council, the Labor Board, the P.T.A. Council, the Y.W.C.A., the Dayton Council, the Boy Scout Council, and the Masons and Order of the Eastern Star.   Using the Spearman rank correlation coefficient to determine the amount of agreement between the rankings by the two groups, *rho* was found to have a value of .58.   The test for significance of association disclosed the value of t to be 2.349, which was significant at the .05 level.   Therefore, the Spearman correlation indicates a fairly significant association between the rankings by the Negro leader respondents and minority community respondents.

Only 5.1 per cent of the sub-community sample proved unable to identify the ten most influential sub-community organizations, and only 1.2 per cent of its votes went to other organizations, as compared to 2.5 per cent of the votes of the Negro leaders.   An analysis by class reveals

1. See, for example, Edward Suchman, *et al., Desegregation: Some Propositions and Research Suggestions* (New York: Anti-Defamation League of B'nai B'rith, 1958).

a significant awareness of the most influential community
organizations at each class level:

Sub-Community Votes by Class

	Upper	Middle	Lower
Top Ten Organizations	97.0%	95.0%	88.4%
Other Organizations	1.3	0.8	1.8
Don't Know	1.7	4.2	9.8
TOTAL	100.0	100.0	100.0

Of special interest is the fact that, while over 40 per cent
of the lower class could not identify their community leaders, the vast majority recognized the community structures
through which the leaders operated.

Of those sub-community respondents queried (54 per
cent), 32 per cent were members of one or more of the
top organizations, and 46 per cent were members of groups
affiliated with these organizations.   This compares with
the 93.8 per cent of those in the Negro leader poll who
were members of at least one of the ten associations, with
an average of three memberships per leader.[2]

All class groups held membership in the N.A.A.C.P.
Upper- and middle-class respondents listed the Crescent
Negro Council and the P.T.A. more frequently than did
lower-class respondents.   Middle- and lower-class informants were more likely to belong to labor organizations—
only two upper-class respondents were affiliated with the
Labor Board.   Middle and lower classes belonged to the
Y's and the neighborhood councils more frequently than
did the upper class.   The Negro Business League was
listed most often by the upper class, although some middle-
class respondents claimed membership.   The League is

2. The 31 power nominees were all members of at least one of
the ten associations, with an average of 3.6 memberships per leader.
This compares with an average of 4.1 memberships in Negro community organizations in general.

made up of professionals—teachers, lawyers, doctors, college administrators—and Negro businessmen, and thus cuts across the upper and middle classes. The 1959 president, for example, was a service station owner and operator.

Nearly 50 per cent of the total number of votes cast by sub-community respondents asked to identify influential Negro organizations went to the Crescent Negro Council, the N.A.A.C.P., and the Negro Business League. Among the leaders, these three groups received 53 per cent of the total number of votes. Leaders rated the Crescent Negro Council and the Negro Business League higher than the N.A.A.C.P. The average citizen, on the other hand, considered the Negro Council and the N.A.A.C.P. more important than the Business League. The N.A.A.C.P. was rated first by the lower-class Negro, and second, by one vote, by the middle-class Negro. The two groups receiving the largest number of votes from the Negro citizenry are important protest organizations. Membership in them is open to the community at large, and, though their policies are formulated by committees composed of influential leaders, the public does have a voice in the basic decisions.

The more important of the two is the Crescent Negro Council. Here leaders come together as problems arise and through standing committees, or *ad hoc* committees comprised of representatives from the Council and other organizations, reach appropriate decisions. Leaders often operate informally at the initial stages of an issue, and discussions of basic problems at luncheon meetings or other informal gatherings are common. Eventually issues reach the organized structure of the Council, when citizens at large have an opportunity to voice their opinions and suggestions. The bimonthly meetings of the Council may have from 50 to 75 persons in attendance, simply as interested citizens. While most are representatives of upper and middle classes, members of the lower class are always present.

About 25 to 30 per cent of those in attendance are women. All present have a vote. It is in this way that leaders and individual citizens keep abreast of community sentiment.

Negro leaders were asked what channels of communication were most effective between the leaders and the sub-community. They listed, in order, the churches, the Crescent Negro Council, the N.A.A.C.P., the Business League, the P.T.A.'s, the Ministerial Council, and the Negro newspaper. Over 85 per cent believed that the lines of interaction between the leaders and the total Negro population were good and improving. They considered that they made concerted efforts to discover what the opinions of the public were and that they also attempted to communicate their own attitudes to the people. While most leaders indicated that it was difficult to reach much of the lower class, they did believe that significant headway had been made in recent years in this respect.

Informants in the sub-community sample were asked about their relationships with their power-leader nominees. Fourteen per cent of the upper class, 29 per cent of the middle class, and 60 per cent of the lower class failed to respond to this question. For those responding, the upper class had an average of .92 periodic contacts per leader, the middle class an average of .5 such contacts per leader, and the lower class an average of only .2 contacts per leader. It should be recalled that not all the votes cast by the sub-community went to the 31 power nominees, and contacts with lesser community leaders are therefore not included in this analysis.

Contacts were defined for the informants in terms of major organizational structures and more personal relationships. The informants who responded to the question interacted most frequently with leaders at the business level— that is, either they worked for, traded or banked with, or sought business advice from their leader selections. Some

29.8 per cent of the contacts in all classes were of this nature. Approximately 29.2 per cent of the relationships in all classes were of a personal nature. Informants having such relationships went to the leaders for advice and counsel about a wide variety of matters—family, health, religious, and occupational. Civil and associational interaction accounted for 11.2 per cent of the relationships between respondents and power nominees. Social interaction—visits in the home, attendance at the same social affairs or membership in the same social organizations—was responsible for 11.6 per cent of these contacts. Miscellaneous contacts—shared church membership, common area of residence, and friendships of sons and daughters—accounted for 16.2 per cent of the relationships, and 1.3 per cent of the contacts were sustained through family ties.

The upper class, as might be expected, had significantly more frequent social, civic, and family contacts with their leaders than did either the middle or lower classes, and the same difference obtained between the middle class and the lower class. Contacts between members of the lower class and the top leaders were largely business or personal.

The possibility that informants selected as power leaders persons with whom they had some interaction, rather than the actual leaders, was reflected among the lower class respondents, who chose residual leaders far more frequently than did members of other classes. The significant relationship between the community-sample leader choices and the selections by Negro and white leaders does indicate, however, that the majority of the respondents selected those they perceived to be actual power figures.[3]

The interaction between power leaders and lesser leaders

3. The large numbers of female respondents undoubtedly distorted responses to queries about contacts with leaders and about community organizations, since women are as a rule much less active in civic affairs than men in Crescent City's minority community.

has been discussed throughout this study. Channels between the power leaders and the citizen are more limited, but do exist nevertheless. It is, of course, unlikely that any power leaders will interact broadly with large numbers of citizens, but in the Crescent sub-community organizational avenues are available so that the leaders and the Negro population at large may impinge upon one another.

It is true that many citizens of the sub-community, particularly in the lower class, do lack contact with their leaders and the organizational activities surrounding community issues. Some few lack the church affiliation that provides a tie to the whole minority community. Others belong to the small sects that refuse to attach themselves to the basic structures represented in the Ministerial Council. Some 40 per cent of the lower class were unable to name any of the community leaders. This lack of communication stands as evidence of the need to raise the socio-economic levels of this group, but it is not evidence of any tendency on the part of the leaders to keep their people ignorant of community affairs.

But communication lines are open for the more articulate at several levels, with the basic sub-community organizations serving as centers of power. By working through the most influential of these organizations, leaders maintain contact with their active followers and the sub-community as a whole. The leaders are recognized. Responsibility can be determined when decisions fail to meet the expectations of the sub-community, and approval can be accorded when the goals of the general citizenry are achieved.

Similarity between the attitudes of the leaders and of their followers indicates the presence of communication on specific issues. The positive stand of the leaders with regard to civil rights has given the community new courage.

Community interest serves as an added incentive to the leaders in their fight for equality.

I wanted especially to learn what the Negro leaders felt was the Negro attitude toward desegregation. The more active the leader, it appeared, the more likely he was to see the general citizenry as favoring desegregation.

Leader Perception of Negro Community Attitudes
Toward Desegregation

	Power Leaders	Power Nominees	Lesser Leaders
Difficult to know	5.4%	8.7%	7.4%
Apathetic	17.0	17.4	29.6
Divided opinion	11.0	17.4	16.7
In favor	66.6	56.5	46.3
TOTAL	100.0	100.0	100.0

Power leaders, in the forefront of the battle, tended to feel that the masses favored an end to segregated patterns. Presumably, active participation had brought them into closer contact with the Negro community. The lesser leaders, who were less committed to the issues, were more likely to feel that the Negroes were apathetic. Several expressed the belief that apathy about desegregation was the result of fear of reprisal.

Sub-community informants were asked an open-end question in the hope that it would elicit their actual attitudes about desegregation. Over 63 per cent of those queried favored desegregation of schools and other community facilities without qualification. Fourteen per cent were ambivalent. Some who opposed desegregation of the schools because it would be "hard on the Negro children" favored desegregation of other areas of community life. Ten and four-tenths per cent of the respondents refused to express their views; 3.6 per cent claimed they knew nothing about the issue. The remaining 8.6 per cent expressed opposition to desegregation at any level.   Some insisted that the Negro was not ready for integration.   Others said that violence would occur if Negroes pressed for desegregation of the schools.

TABLE 12
SUB-COMMUNITY ATTITUDES TOWARD DESEGREGATION, BY CLASS

Attitudes	PERCENTAGE HOLDING ATTITUDE			
	Upper Class	Middle Class	Lower Class	Total Sample
Against	1.2	10.7	13.1	8.6
Refused to Express Views	11.6	3.2	16.1	10.4
Knew Nothing about Issue	——	4.3	6.1	3.6
Ambivalent Toward Issue	8.1	14.0	19.3	14.0
In Favor: Gradualism	15.1	20.5	10.1	15.2
In Favor: Immediately	64.0	47.3	35.3	48.2
TOTAL	100.0	100.0	100.0	100.0

Most of those favoring desegregation were concerned with the improvement of economic opportunities for the Negro.   Desegregation of schools and other facilities was regarded as a positive way of breaking economic barriers. This tends also to be the Negro leaders' belief.

The class analysis in Table 12 shows that 79.1 per cent of the upper class favored desegregation, compared to 67.8 per cent of the middle class and 45.4 per cent of the lower class.   The middle- and lower-class informants supporting desegregation tended to offer ethical and religious reasons for integration.   The upper class preferred legal and constitutional arguments.[4]

4. It is likely that responses on this question, especially, were distorted. The interviewers in the sub-community were white. Negro respondents were less likely to express dissatisfaction with basic institutional patterns to white interviewers than to Negro interviewers. Furthermore, the interviewers were often members of a higher class than those interviewed, and an element of reticence probably proceeded from this difference as well.   For a recent discussion of the problems of

I wanted, in addition, to determine the degree of community approval of the leaders' actions. A seven-point scale was used to determine levels of agreement or disagreement. The results of this analysis are represented, by class, in Table 13.

TABLE 13

AMOUNT OF AGREEMENT WITH OPINIONS AND ACTIONS OF NEGRO LEADERS ON DESEGREGATION ISSUES, AS INDICATED BY SUB-COMMUNITY SAMPLE

Agreement-Disagreement	PERCENTAGE OF AGREEMENT			
	Upper Class	Middle Class	Lower Class	Total Sample
Agree Stongly	45.9	26.0	19.4	29.7
Agree Moderately	34.1	25.0	15.3	24.4
Agree Slightly	4.7	9.0	5.1	6.5
Don't Know	12.9	30.0	50.0	31.6
Disagree Slightly	2.4	5.0	2.0	3.2
Disagree Moderately	——	2.0	——	0.6
Disagree Strongly	——	3.0	8.2	4.0
TOTAL	100.0	100.0	100.0	100.0

Approximately 61 per cent of the respondents expressed at least minimum agreement with the leaders' actions; 54.1 per cent of these were moderately or strongly in agreement. Only 7.8 per cent voiced disapproval, with the remaining 31.6 per cent unable or unwilling to commit themselves. The respondents who favored desegregation approved of the actions and decisions of the Crescent City Negro leaders. Those opposed to desegregation were in disagreement with the leaders. The observations in this instance were therefore consistent with earlier observations.

Nearly 85 per cent of the upper-class respondents, 60 per cent of the middle-class respondents, and 40 per cent

---

racial and class bias in interviewing, see Gerhard E. Lenski and John C. Leggett, "Caste, Class, and Deference in the Research Interview," *American Journal of Sociology*, LXV (March, 1960), pp. 463-67.

of the lower-class respondents showed agreement with the actions of the leaders.   Only 2.4 per cent, 10 per cent, and 10.2 per cent, respectively, reflected disagreement.   Of those who were not in accord, 2.4 per cent of the upper class and 2 per cent of the middle class felt the leaders were not active enough in promoting desegregation.   The remainder in disagreement contended that the leaders were too active.

Fifty per cent of the lower class informants did not know whether they agreed or disagreed with the leaders' actions.   This statistic reflects the inability of some 40 per cent of these informants to identify the leaders in the Negro community.   But of the lower-class respondents who were conversant with the leaders' actions, agreement is greater than disagreement by 4 to 1.

This variation by class was expected.   My findings also confirmed those of John Haer, who found that persons ranking highest on the social scale have the most favorable attitudes toward the actions of community leaders.[5]

It is, then, the more articulate upper- and middle-class group which wields the most influence upon the leaders and the community power structure.   But even among the lower-class respondents who expressed their views, there was significantly more agreement with desegregation and the actions of the sub-community leaders than there was disagreement.   The evidence in Crescent City does not support those who feel that Negro leaders are out of touch with the Negro masses.[6]

Unlike some other communities, Crescent City has a Negro leadership that is aggressive and informed to the point that it is, as a group, ahead of the masses in its willing-

5. John L. Haer, "Social Stratification in Relation to Attitudes Toward Sources of Power in a Community," *Social Forces,* 35 (December, 1956), 140-42.

6. See, for example, Hugh Smythe, "Negro Masses and Leaders, Characteristics: An Analysis of Current Trends," *Sociology and Social Research,* 35 (1950), 31-37.

ness to work for the rights of the Negro community. In Crescent there is no sharp split between the accommodative and protest leaders such as exists in Tallahassee, Florida.[7]

The Negro community of Crescent City is a functional sub-system of the entire metropolis. A sub-structure of power as well as a sub-community, it is interlocked with the organization and structure of the larger community. In the past, though a few of the Negro leaders worked with some of the white leaders on an informal but accommodating basis, in general the minority citizens and their leaders were isolated from the power structure of the white community because of their lack of access to the institutions and associations of the dominant group. Gradually these barriers have been breaking down, with the result that Negroes have gained access to community-wide policy-making organizations.

Of course the very nature of the minority community's position as such has meant that Negro power and decision-making has been influenced by the attitudes and actions of the white-community leaders. Yet in recent years this influence has become less potent, and the avenues for the exercise of a reciprocal influence over the white community leaders have been strengthened.

To obtain some objective notion of the relationships existing between the Negro and white leadership, both groups of informants were asked a series of questions about interaction and communication between the two segments of the biracial community. Both groups identified two avenues of contact—the more formal institutional and organizational channels, and informal and sometimes more covert face-to-face meetings between leaders of the two groups.

Formal institutional and organizational structures which

7. Lewis Killian and Charles U. Smith, "Negro Protest Leaders in a Southern Community," *Social Forces*, 38 (March, 1960), 253-57.

the Negro leadership considered the best avenues of communication between the two groups were of several kinds. Some were economic—business associations, especially in banking, insurance, and finance, the Committee for Industrial and Economic Expansion and its affiliated Crescent Industrial Development Corporation, the Urban Renewal Board, the Board of Adjustment, labor unions, and professional organizations. Some were political—the parties, in particular the Crescent County Democratic and Republican Executive Committees, and the City Council. Some were civic—the United Fund committees and board, the Crescent Youth Board, the Social Planning Council, the Commission on Race Relations, Family Service, Girl and Boy Scout Councils, and a large number of other community services and welfare agencies. Some were religious —biracial ministerial organizations and the Friends Service Committee. And some were educational—the local and state school boards, and college and university biracial committees and activities.

Those interviewed in the Negro leader poll were asked to record the number of local biracial associations and committees of which they had been members, and the number of local interracial executive or advisory boards on which they had served, during three years preceding. The respondents had belonged to an average of 1.8 biracial organizations or committees and .93 biracial community boards in that time, distributed through 30 biracial associations. Of the power leaders, all but four were active in biracial organizations. As a group they belonged to an average of 2.2 local biracial associations or committees and 1.2 executive or advisory boards. These figures do not include state and national memberships. Respondents in the Negro leader poll held memberships in an average of 1.7 state biracial groups and 1.8 national biracial groups.

The responses of the white leaders with respect to the

best lines of communication between the two races corresponded rather closely to those of the Negro leaders. White leaders mentioned 17 economic, political, religious, and civic associations which they felt to be especially effective. The more important of these groups, according to the white informants, were the Committee for Industrial and Economic Expansion, the Democratic Party and its Executive Committee, the City Council, the United Fund and other social-agency groups, and the Commission on Race Relations. In 1958 a very small majority of the white leaders approved of the Commission on Race Relations, and a number of them were undecided about its effectiveness. By the spring of 1959, however, all but five of the white leaders regarded it as a promising instrument for interracial progress.

All but three of the white leader informants shared one or more biracial memberships with Negro leaders. As a group they served on an average of 2.9 biracial associations and boards. They interacted regularly with 14 of the Negro power leaders in these organizations. They had periodic contact with the others, as well as with many individuals in the sub-structure of Negro leadership.

Some Negro representation in the organizational life of the larger community is merely token. And some of the major policy groups, such as the Chamber of Commerce and the Merchants' Association, are still blocked to Negroes. Yet they have become involved in a significant number of important community structures. Their participation is increasing, not only in the less powerful of the associational groupings, but also in the more important policy-making boards and executive committees. They have been most successful at the political, civic, and community-welfare levels, but they have gained an entrance to the economic, educational, and religious areas as well.

Informal lines of communication were regarded as vital

in the communication process by a majority of the white leaders. Seventy-five per cent indicated that they met informally from time to time with the Negro leaders. They were asked to give the names of others in the white community who they felt interacted most frequently with Negro leaders on problems of mutual concern. Twenty-two white leaders received the majority of votes. All but five of the white leaders interviewed in the study were included among them. Of this group of 22, only three did not appear on the list of 37 perceived primary and secondary white leaders in Crescent City compiled in a study of Mid-South State urban centers carried on in 1958.[8] Fourteen of the white leaders identified by the researcher's white informants were also mentioned by the Negro leaders.

We noted in the last chapter the way in which informal contacts were made on specific issues. Often personal meetings between Negro and white leaders occur in their business offices. Interestingly enough, such visits are made either by white leaders to Negro offices or by Negro leaders to white offices. Such visits are somewhat covert, but they are becoming less so. As one white power leader put it, "I have no hesitation in going to them, and they don't hesitate to call on me." Phone calls and personal notes or letters are also exchanged between individuals. Occasionally biracial meetings are held in the directors' offices of one of the white banks, insurance firms, or other leading financial institutions. Although the leaders seldom meet over lunch, they have done so. From time to time informal meetings take place with a few of the leaders of both races in the Beta Dining Room, operated by the Negro insurance and banking firms.

Evidence supports the belief that channels of com-

8. Unpublished research by the Urban Studies Committee of the Institute for Research in Social Science, University of North Carolina. Permission to quote data granted by the Director of the Urban Studies Committee.

munication between the two elements of the community
have actually broadened within the past decade, at least
as far as formal organizational structures are concerned.
It is significant, therefore, that nearly 40 per cent of the
Negro leaders and 35 per cent of the white leaders sensed
that channels of communication were not as free since
1954, when the desegregation movement began in earnest.
Several respondents in both racial groups noted a very
plausible explanation in their interviews.

First of all, many of the issues of present concern to
the Negro leaders are related to attempts to break segregated patterns within the community. Most of the white
leaders have been hesitant to discuss such matters openly
with the minority community. The behavior of the school
board in the matter of school desegregation is a case in
point. Most biracial associations have attempted to steer
clear of controversial discussion.

Closely related to this shift in the type of issue is a
shift in the type of Negro leadership and its approach to
the white leaders. The minority leaders with whom the
whites deal are no longer emissaries seeking such concessions as the white community may be willing to grant.
The Negroes now bargain from a more secure position.
They go to the whites only with concrete demands. In
many cases, indeed, they no longer seek the support of
white leaders, but seek to achieve their ends in other ways.
Neither the Negro nor the white position in interracial
affairs is as flexible now; there is less room for compromise. Consequently, a change in pattern of informal communication has occurred. Because white leaders have been
unable or unwilling to accept these changes in relative
strength, some types of intercourse have diminished or
disappeared completely.

The more progressive white power leaders, who outnum-
ber the conservatives, show less reticence about meeting

with Negroes on a nearly equal footing. Many of them feel
that interaction is still present and is even increasing slightly, in spite of the controversial issues facing the community today.   One of the white leaders expressed it this
way: "I don't think channels of communication are more
restricted than they were prior to the fifty-four decision.
I think lines of demarcation have been more sharply drawn.
Room for compromise and objective discussion has de-
creased. The Negro position is less fluid, as is the white.
But the channels are still there, and more of us in both
groups are attempting to use them."

Howard Adams, one of the top Negro power figures,
had this to say early in 1959: "I was discouraged in 1957.
It seemed that the lines were practically closed as far as
discussing desegregation was concerned. But things are
better now. We have more people to sit down and talk
with—white leaders who know the score, understand it,
and are willing to act. These are informal contacts mostly,
but they are beginning to pay off. And the make-up of
the City Council has helped a great deal."

While it cannot be said that there is a free flow of
information between the two groups, the flow is considerably less restricted than some students of the biracial
power situation have thought. Both racial groups withhold information in order to maintain bargaining power.
This is to be expected. But in Crescent City, at least,
there seems to be a somewhat more honest exchange than
is found in many other biracial settings.

Some rather surprising facts were reflected in the white
informants' attitudes toward the top Negro leadership.
For example, 65 per cent of the white leaders had
attitudes of respect toward the top Negro leaders. As one
of the most powerful white leaders and economic dominants expressed it, "The top leadership in our Negro community is stable, dignified, and responsible. We are for-

tunate in having people who are among the finest Negro leaders in the state."

Donald Boyd, a member of the conservative Cranston family, is considered to be among the more reactionary whites by many of his more liberal peers. But there are indications that Boyd has altered his stand on race relations. His remarks may exemplify the kind of subtle change that is occurring. In spring, 1959, he indicated that he felt quite encouraged about race relations in the city. When asked about white leaders with whom the Negroes interacted on an informal basis, Boyd replied, "I would like to be thought of as one who is now sympathetic to some of the aspirations of this group. I know I am not so considered, but I'm trying to do something about it—to mend my fences. Negroes can rightly ask, 'What does Boyd want from us? What are his ulterior motives?' I have none. I just realize that it's time we changed."

Another top white leader gave this illustration of the kinds of shifts that are beginning to occur within Crescent City: "Early in 1950 Negro leaders began pushing for representation on the city fire department. When discussion reached the City Council, Roger Cranston, one of the wealthiest and most conservative business men here, contacted the city fathers and the fire department and 'suggested' that the firemen refuse to train Negroes. The matter was dropped. But in 1957 the Negroes got Negro fireman appointments passed through the Council. The progressive leadership worked with the fire department, and there was no trouble. A number of Negroes were trained without incident."

If the contacts I have described were really superficial and ineffective, there might be three results. First, there would be little recognition in either group of the most powerful leaders in the opposition. The evidence in chapter IV does not support this assumption. There is among both races agreement on the identity of the leaders of both races. Second, little exertion of significant influence on basic community issues by the minority leadership might be anticipated. This assumption, too, as I have noted earlier, does not obtain. Third, little acquaintance in either group with the aspirations and attitudes of the other on issues such as school desegregation might be expected. White leaders might be expected to believe that the majority of Negroes in Crescent City do not really want to change "southern traditions" and that radicals from the N.A.A.C.P. or from the "outside" are responsible for the agitation. Negro leaders might see in the vocal and extreme pro-segregation minority the reflection of the sentiments of the entire white community and might accordingly be expected to be apprehensive about violence, reprisals, and other extreme tactics.

One way of testing the third supposition is to examine the attitudes of white leaders on school desegregation to determine whether there was any significant amount of communication between them and Negro leaders on this issue. I found that 25 per cent of the white leaders believed the community should submit to the law of the land and desegregate the schools. Twenty per cent were strongly opposed to desegregation and willing to block it regardless of consequences. The remaining 55 per cent fell somewhere between these two groups. They did not favor school desegregation, but believed that it was inevitable. They did not believe that positive action against it was wise or necessary, and they felt that when it came it would be accepted calmly. The first two groups are composed of the most liberal and the most conservative white leaders. In the last and largest group are the moderate or progressive white leaders of Crescent City. It is their approach to the issue that has been reflected in the action, or more accurately the lack of action, of the white community. The Mayor voiced the sentiment of the moderates in these words: "I believe most of the white leaders feel that the best way for school desegregation to come is through the courts, with the Negroes rather than whites pushing for it. A lot of pro-integration people here feel that if it comes legally the people in the city will respect it more. Many not in favor of it, but not violently opposed, feel the same way. We've got a lot of lower- and laboring-class whites here that many leaders think have to be appeased. The school board seems the least willing to gamble, so it is holding the line on segregation."

Included in the Urban Studies Committee research cited previously was a series of questions concerning attitudes toward school segregation-desegregation policies, patterned after the work of Tumin.[9] Both white leaders and a white community sample were asked to select one of four alternative courses to be followed in the event of school desegregation: amend the Constitution to remove school segregation from the jurisdiction of the Supreme Court; withhold state funds from school districts which desegregate; close the schools; resist desegregation by force, if necessary. The results showed that both the white leaders and the white citizens of Crescent City[10] were substantially more disposed to preserve the public school system in spite of desegregation than to alter it to preserve segregation. The leaders evidenced somewhat more liberal attitudes than did the general public. The following statistics detail the white leaders' attitudes toward alternative courses of action with regard to school desegregation:

9. Melvin M. Tumin, *Desegregation: Resistance and Readiness* (Princeton, N. J.: Princeton University Press, 1958).

10. Fifty-five white leaders were included in this poll; 37 of them represented the "perceived top and secondary leadership structure" from which the white-leader informants for my study were drawn. Eighteen of the white-leader informants in the Urban Study Committee research were economic dominants who did not fall in the top or secondary leadership category. This latter group was found to be the most strongly segregationist of the white leaders.

| White Leaders | Segregation-Desegregation Attitudes | | | |
	Amend Constitution	Withhold State Funds	Close Schools	Use Force
Approve	70%	18%	20%	2%
Undecided	5	16	14	9
Disapprove	25	64	66	89

Interestingly, the "perceived top leaders" were even more opposed to actions jeopardizing the public school system than were the other leaders. Eighty-two per cent disapproved of withholding state funds or closing the schools in Crescent City in case of desegregation. All of them opposed violence in any form.[11]

These responses correspond to the attitudes I found among the informants in the white sample. The liberal leaders who felt Crescent City should submit to the law of the land correspond to the 25 per cent of the Urban Study Committee respondents who opposed a constitutional amendment as well as other alternative courses of action. The extreme segregationists who were opposed to school desegregation regardless of consequences are reflected in the 18 and 20 per cent of the Urban Center's sample who favored closing schools or withholding funds, as well as in the 2 per cent who favored violence. The moderate attitude of the majority of white leaders corresponds to the strong vote opposing the withholding of funds, closing of schools, or violence. Thus, while there is an extreme pro-segregation element within the white leadership of Crescent City, it is opposed by a considerably larger number of moderate leaders.

The Urban Studies Committee reported that 75 per

11. Unpublished research by the Urban Studies Committee of the Institute for Research in Social Science.

cent of the leaders it interviewed were interested in working with problems related to school desegregation but
fewer than 30 per cent of the top and secondary leaders
were actually actively participating. Among the more conservative, pro-segregationist leaders, 44 per cent had worked
against desegregation.[12] This stratum of leaders and economic dominants comprises, in part, the membership of
the Crescent Public Education Committee which evolved
about 1956 in reaction to school desegregation. Most of the
white informants I interviewed suggested that the group
was composed of business, labor, and rural factions who
have had but one thing in common—their anti-Negro
sentiments. "They are a relatively unorganized, highly militant lunatic fringe," according to Richard Bosworth, president of the Piedmont National Bank. "They are extrem-
ists who wouldn't be seen together ordinarily. They've had
support from some of the reactionary industrialists and
financiers, and they are the only group that has openly
opposed school desegregation. But they fell apart after
their defeat at the polls in 1957. We don't hear as much
from them any more."

A few groups—some of the faculty at Southern University, the League of Women Voters, The American
Friends Service Committee, the American Association of
University Women—and a few isolated individuals took
a positive stand, but most preferred to remain silent. I
was interested in the reasons for this general passive position on an issue of such importance and asked the white
leaders about it.

Their responses by and large mirrored their own attitudes toward the quality of leadership in the white community. Fifty-five per cent thought that Crescent City
suffered from a lack of strong white leadership. One leader stated it in this way: "Crescent City hasn't had as much

12. *Ibid.*

farsighted leadership in the past as have some of the cities around here. We've been a community of factions, and this has been exposed in the lack of action regarding school desegregation. A little shot of dynamic leadership would help a lot in uniting and moving the progressives."

The Negroes were well aware of the sentiments and activities of the extreme anti-Negro group of white leaders. However, they did not believe that this extreme view represented the position of the majority of white leaders. I asked Negro leaders if active opposition to school desegregation had affected their policies or activities. Approximately 49 per cent felt that there had been no effect at all. Thirty-two per cent estimated that such opposition had only served to make the Negro leadership more determined. Only 19 per cent acknowledged that such white opposition had made some Negroes, especially the conservatives, more timid.

Over 90 per cent of the Negro leaders believed that there would be no violence, no economic reprisals, and no closing of the schools as a result of school integration. A great many pointed out that their contacts with the more moderate white leaders convinced them that extreme tactics would not be used. But the minority leaders manifested a great deal of impatience with the lack of positive white leadership. They, too, felt that Crescent City lacked a strong nucleus of progressive white leaders who were willing to initiate action. One Negro leader explained it this way: "We'll have to keep pushing, pushing, pushing to get what we want. There is too much fear of being labeled pro-Negro if whites take a positive or open stand on desegregation issues. What we have to do is maneuver some of the more moderate whites into taking progressive action on race relations—that's going to be our policy from now on." It has been the moderate white leader, with whom the Negro leadership has more often had contact in recent years, who has no doubt influenced the policies and actions of the Negro leaders most significantly. It is possible, therefore, that Negroes discerned less extreme hostility toward school desegregation and related issues than actually existed within the white community.

The white leaders' recognition of Negro attitudes and aspirations was also rather striking. A majority of the white informants were anti-N.A.A.C.P. Yet only 25 per cent of those interviewed asserted that the majority of Negro leaders were being led by N.A.A.C.P. radicals. Seventy-five per cent felt that all Negro leaders were behind the push to end segregation in schools. They viewed the efforts of the Crescent Negro Council and the political behavior of the minority community as being dedicated to this end. Many of the white informants said that, from what they had been able to gather from conversations with Negroes, the sub-community was going to continue to demand a greater voice in community affairs. One white insurance executive said, "Don't kid yourself. Those boys are going to keep trying—they won't stop with integrated schools. I can tell that by talking to them. They haven't got too far on this school business yet, but they have been pretty successful and they've been rewarded with considerable response in the past few years."

It is not my intention to paint an idealistic picture of race relations in Crescent City. The community still has a long way to go. Old fears and prejudices still dominate much of the thinking. Strong anti-Negro feelings are voiced by a noisy minority. The moderate white leader's role is in no sense that of acquiescing to Negro demands. There is a genuine commitment to maintaining a degree of white supremacy. But the community has come much further than many other urban centers of the South. Placed on a continuum it would undoubtedly rank higher than many other cities with respect to its race relations. And the quality of the Negro leadership has played a decisive role in bringing this situation about.

Power leaders of the sub-community have access to many of their white counterparts. There is a significant awareness of the leadership structure on both sides; the attitudes and aspirations of each group are not unknown to the other. Communication and interaction channels do operate at more than a superficial level between the two leadership structures.

CHAPTER VII

MINORITY POWER AND RACE
LEADERSHIP

N O study of minority community power is completely in-
telligible without some attention given to types of race
leaders. Types of Negro leadership have been touched upon
only incidentally in studies of Negro power structures by
Hunter, and Barth and Abu Laban. Changes in race and
power relations in Crescent City have made very clear the
new roles of race leaders and power leaders in the Negro
community.

Much of the literature on American Negro leadership
has in the past concerned itself with "race-leader" typologies. The "accommodating" versus the "protest" dichot-
omy has been most popular. In 1937 Guy B. Johnson
characterized Negro leadership as "gradualist" and "rev-
olutionary."[1] Myrdal has described the accommodating,
compromise, and protest leaders. Similar typologies have
been developed by Drake and Cayton, Cox, and others.[2]

1. Guy B. Johnson, "Negro Racial Movements and Leadership in the
United States," *American Journal of Sociology,* XLIII (July, 1937),
57-71.
2. Gunnar Myrdal, *An American Dilemma* (2 vols.; New York:
Harper and Brothers, 1944); St. Clair Drake and H. R. Cayton, *Black
Metropolis* (New York: Harcourt, Brace and Co., 1945); Oliver Cox,
"Leadership Among Negroes in the United States," in *Studies in Leadership,* ed. A. W. Gouldner (New York: Harper and Brothers, 1950),
pp. 228-70. A discussion of Robert Johnson's recent typology of "Negro
social types" has not been included here because he is not primarily concerned with leadership. While two of his categories, the "race man" and
the "interracial duty squad," have some reference to types of leaders, the
over-all typology represents minority attitudes and behavior toward

Frazier feels, however, that changes in the relation of the Negro to the American community suggest a more significant classification of leaders than that provided by pure "race-leader" typologies. A functional typology which also takes into account the increasing literacy and the resulting differentiation of economic and cultural interests is indicated, especially for the urban South and the North.[3]

For the purposes of my study, I hypothesized, on the basis of certain indications and suggestions in the literature, that the Negro role as power leader cannot be separated from the role as race leader. The hypothesis has two corollaries—that within the Negro leadership structure there exists a diversity of race-leader types identifiable by the leader's stand on desegregation, and that the desegregation issue will result in a shift in power from certain types of race leaders to others. The observations in Crescent City substantiate the hypothesis.

The pilot study in Crescent City revealed that individual leaders tended to rank themselves and their peers in terms of a fourfold classification—radical, liberal, moderate, and conservative.[4] Respondents to the Negro leader poll were asked to characterize themselves and other lead-

---

whites rather than leadership roles. See Robert Johnson, "Negro Reaction to Minority Group Status," in *American Minorities,* ed. Milton L. Barron (New York: Alfred A. Knopf, 1957), pp. 192-212.

3. E. Franklin Frazier, *The Negro in the United States* (New York: The Macmillan Co., 1949), pp. 554-63.

4. With the arrival of the Black Muslims in Crescent City in 1961, the possibility for yet another type of Negro leader has presented itself. The local organization heads, Izu Karien and Kenneth X., are vigorous and dedicated Muslims, following closely the ultra-radical tenets of the nation-wide movement. They hope to attract a large number of the sub-community's citizens, especially those from the lower class, who, according to Muslim leaders, have been less thoroughly "brainwashed" by white culture than have members of the Negro middle and upper classes. Should the Black Muslims prove as successful in Crescent City as they have in some communities, they may eventually become contenders for leadership and power within the sub-community. See C. Eric Lincoln, *The Black Muslims in America* (Boston: Beacon Press, 1961).

ers in terms of general policies and specifically in terms of racial issues. The determinant was found to be the approach to racial issues, but the classification obtained thereby rarely conflicted with the classification obtained on the basis of the approach to other social problems.

Liberal leaders predominate, as the following figures show:

Type of Leader	RACE-LEADER PEER GROUP CLASSIFICATION			
	Radical	Liberal	Moderate	Conservative
General Leadership Structure	3.7%	48.1%	35.2%	13.0%
Power Nominees	6.5	54.8	19.4	19.3
Power Leaders	9.1	72.7	18.2	——

While some conservative leaders were still regarded as powerful, none, it was found, any longer plays a decision-making role.

Considerable agreement existed between the individual's self-characterization and the rating by his peers. Among the 31 power nominees, there were only five variations. Three conservatives rated themselves more liberal than did their peers. One was a moderate who rated himself as a liberal; one was a liberal who ranked himself more conservatively than did the other leaders.

Liberal leaders were chosen three times more frequently than conservative leaders as power nominees in the sub-community sample. Leaders selected as being active in community issue areas were also found to be more liberal. "Issue" leaders for school desegregation were liberal six to one over conservatives and three to one over moderates. The majority of those regarded as most powerful by both the minority leaders and the general citizenry are liberals active in all phases of desegregation.

When leaders were asked what part they played in the desegregation issue, 59 per cent said they had been active. Twenty-three, or 79.3 per cent of those who claimed to have been active, appeared among the power nominees. Twenty were observed to be active decision-makers. Approximately 61 per cent of the leaders interviewed said they had been asked by others to work on desegregation problems. Thirty-nine per cent of all leaders had contacted others on the issue. All but one of these appeared among the power nominees, and 75 per cent of those who contacted others proved to be power leaders.

When the leaders were asked what individuals were most active in working for desegregation, the 31 power nominees received the overwhelming number of votes. Those identified as decision-makers in the case analysis of issues headed the list. Some 79.8 per cent of the persons selected by the Negro leader poll as being most active in desegregation were tagged as radical or liberal leaders. Eighteen per cent were regarded as moderates, and only 2.2 per cent were considered conservatives by their peers.

In order to uncover shifts in leadership since 1954, the investigator asked the respondents in the Negro leader poll which leaders had lost influence because of their stand on school desegregation. Some 36.7 per cent of the respondents felt that none of the influential leaders had lost power since 1954. An additional 25.6 per cent qualified their negative answers by indicating that conservative Negro leadership in Crescent City had begun to lose power prior to 1954. This group felt, accordingly, that there had been an increase in the stature of such liberals as Adams, McDonald, Healy, Sherwood, Erickson, Hale, and Wareman.

Approximately 47 per cent thought that some leaders had lost influence because of conservativism on desegregation. Listed most frequently as having lost power were

Albert French, T. O. Bradock, the Reverend Allen Kyser, Ruth Johnson, Miles Conners, and Winston Arthur—all considered to be conservative by their peers. Nathan Banks, considered a moderate leader, was believed by five persons to have lost influence because of his early statements about school desegregation. Three of these suggested that he was regaining his power. Three persons thought Art Troop had lost standing because of his impulsive approach to the issue. Two said that Healy and Sherwood had lost influence among white leaders and conservative Negroes but were gaining among most Negroes. Several lesser community leaders, especially ministers and teachers, were considered timid in their approach to desegregation.

All leaders professed a desire for an end to segregation, but there was a decided difference in their willingness to engage in protest movements. Eight persons in the Negro leader poll were not members of the Crescent Negro Council. Six of these were conservatives; two were moderates. Six individuals, all conservative, were not members of the local N.A.A.C.P. While all other leaders claimed membership in these two most influential protest organizations, degree of participation varied considerably. The radical and liberal leaders were, of course, the most active. Conservatives took only a passive interest in the organizations.

Conservatives are no longer powerful leaders in Crescent City. In the past these compromise leaders often held their positions because they were acceptable to the white community. They believed that the interests of the Negro could best be served by adjusting to the authority of the whites. Some may have feared reprisals if they failed to co-operate with white leaders in controlling the minority community.

They were accepted by other Negroes, not only because accommodation was regarded as the most practical policy, but because they also had prestige in their own right within the Negro social structure. This type of race leader was powerful in Crescent City through the 1930's and early 1940's. Arnold Arthur, Jr., Dr. Stoddard, and Bill Patterson were spokesmen for the Negro community and held a tight rein on sub-community activities.

Today the suggestion that a Negro is unduly susceptible to white influence has meant loss of power. Many of the old leaders are dead; few, if any, leaders conform rigidly to the conservative pattern of accommodation. Conservatives still active in the institutional life have long since lost the right to speak for the Negro. Most of the present-day conservative leaders have been timid in supporting desegregation. They view opposition in the white community as potentially explosive. They describe the Negro masses as apathetic or fearful. Often they suggest that it is impossible to know what the masses want, since the community is seen as being sharply divided.

Conservative leaders still remain the most acceptable to a segment of Crescent City's white leadership. By and large, however, the white leaders by-pass the conservative leader, for they know he no longer wields power in the Negro community. Among the power nominees, French, Conners, Arthur, T. O. Bradock, Swanson, and Kyser represent those who have lost influence and power. Some have become more forthright in their positions on civil rights and therefore still retain a certain prestige; they can, however, no longer command a voice in decision-making. They now "lead" by providing financial support or occasionally by lending a prestigeful name to a special project.

Frazier's discussion of the emergence of a functional Negro leadership is especially significant as applied to the moderate leaders of Crescent City. He suggests that at certain levels a dual focus is essential for the analysis of minority leadership.[5] Certainly in Crescent City it is possible to identify a functional leadership. A more diversified occupational base, the acquisition of political power, and better educational opportunities have resulted in the differentiation of the economic and cultural interests of Negroes residing there. It has therefore been possible for many Negroes to become increasingly integrated into the broader community and national life.

There are those in the sub-community who have chosen to subordinate their role as race leader to their role as functional leader. Devoting their energies to a specialized area of activity, they desire to be known first as successful business executives, academicians, or representatives in regional, national, and international affairs, depending upon the reference group with which they, as individuals, wish to be identified.

Certain upper-class Negroes have retreated from active leadership as a means of isolating themselves from lower-class Negroes and from white discrimination. The functional leaders of Crescent City, however, committed as they are to desegregation, have not retreated. They give strong moral and financial support to protest activities. Occasionally they wield influence behind the scenes by virtue of their ability to delegate community responsibilities to those under them in the institutional structure. But they have been willing to leave to others the responsibilities of local community activity, while they dedicate themselves to more specialized or cosmopolitan pursuits.

The functional leaders are nevertheless classified by their peers as race leaders, and because they have chosen to be vocal in areas other than Negro protest they are considered moderate leaders. Although the functional lead-

5. Frazier, *Negro in the United States*.

er has selected avenues for expressing leadership outside of the basic local issues, he is more active in the community than the conservative leader. Certainly he feels a concern for the masses. But he is more willing to give the white community "buffer time" on racial issues and has considerable faith in the biracial groups attempting to work out joint community problems. Moderate leaders believe that the majority of Negroes in the community, while unwilling to take the initiative on civil rights, are nevertheless eager to follow educated, alert leaders.

With the diminishing influence of the conservative leadership, it was logical that the white leaders should turn to the moderates in their search for "official spokesmen." The power of the moderate leaders was not thereby increased. In most cases moderate leaders have as a means of securing power rejected white approval, for it is as much an obstacle in the way of sub-community leadership for the moderate as for the conservative leader.

Typical of the moderates are Silas Alder, I. N. Karns, Alice Bradock, and Richard Laroux, Sr. Among them, they hold some of the most prestigeful positions in the Negro community. They lend their names to various issues and activities, raise money, are active in support of sub-community policies, and obtain the support of those under their authority. Their power potential is great; that it is not utilized more widely means they have chosen not to play the role of race leader, not to be active decision-makers. It does not mean that they lack influence.

Liberal leaders are younger than the conservative leaders—most liberal leaders are in their late thirties to early fifties. However, they are in no sense new to the community or to the leadership structure. They have resided in Crescent City an average of 25 years. They assumed their leadership soon after World War II. The group includes those who ten or fifteen years ago were considered radical by white leaders.

Comprised largely of economic dominants, small businessmen, and professionals, liberals are outspoken in their approach to social and racial issues. One noticeable shift in the composition of this group is the important part lawyers and educated religious leaders are now playing. There is also wider participation by a small but growing group of college professors. Willing to use a number of means to gain their formal and informal demands—petitions, lawsuits, the ballot, boycotts—they are not above practical bargaining.

The liberal leader, raised in a new tradition, serves as a link between the older leader and the more aggressive and radical race leader who is beginning to emerge. In Crescent City the liberals have been able to add dignity and intelligence to the role of race leader without any compromise of principle. Astute enough to make basic shifts in policy at the appropriate moment, liberal leaders maintain a balance of power. They fight for new proposals, carry out new projects, and rally their followers. They believe that the masses of Negroes are in favor of integration, willing to give wholehearted support to desegregation activities.

Among the liberals, leadership and power are based on militancy, socio-economic standing, personal characteristics, ability to organize, and a sense of genuine responsibility to the entire Negro community. In view of the nature of the leadership they have sought to provide, Crescent liberals have been in a more advantageous position than might have been possible in some other biracial communities. White leaders in Crescent City are more willing to deal with the real Negro leaders. Channels of communication, completely blocked for the protest Negro in some cities, are open in Crescent City. Progressive white leaders now realize they must turn to the liberals because they hold the balance of power, and the whites have accordingly begun to work with this vocal, stable, and sophisticated group of Negroes, more their equals.

The fourth group of race leaders, the radicals, is just emerging. It may join with the liberals as time mellows its members. There is also the possibility that this group will grow in power and strive for control in the future. The present radical leadership is composed of young men in their late twenties and thirties among whom the professions are heavily represented. Many are young ministers just out of divinity school—Martin Luther King is their ideal. Most of them are relatively new to Crescent City. Many are from other parts of the South, and some have attended the local college. They spur on the liberal leaders, keeping them moving with the times.

They want an end to segregation in all areas of life immediately. They are angry young men who prefer boycott and mass demonstration to the slower procedures of arbitration and litigation. In no sense are they a sophisticated or dignified group of leaders. Their appeal to youth is based on their extremely militant stand. They identify with the suppressed Negro masses. They lack the full resources of the Negro community, and so far have gained positions of power only when liberals have voluntarily included them. Denied any such influence, chances are that the radicals would soon upset the balance of power.

Marshall and Troop are the most active radical leaders. Marshall, who is well known, is among the most influential members of the Crescent Negro Council. Orville Robbins, Jake Bronton, and Thurston Polk are also becoming known in leadership circles. Many radicals are motivated by an earnest desire to better the lot of their race, but some of the radical leaders have a strong desire for recognition and

power.   This very desire is likely to stand in their way
in Crescent City, where effective, sincere leadership has always been recognized.

Much has been written about the bases of power.   I
found in Crescent City's minority community that class,
status, family ties, income and wealth, education, organizational position, and personal characteristics are the bases of
leadership.   To these I now must add the value attached to
aggressiveness in the role of racial leader.   The disap-
pearance of the Negro's traditional role and its replacement
by a spirit of equalitarianism have changed the values and
goals held by Negroes everywhere.   It is not surprising,
therefore, to find that the liberal race leader is held in high
esteem by the Negroes in Crescent City.   The new leader
must fight, not acquiesce, if he is to exercise power in the
decision-making process.

My observations confirm Myrdal's thesis that the pattern of Negro leadership in America has always been related to the pattern of race relations.[6]   The power held by
race leaders in Crescent City's Negro community cannot
be separated from their role as such.   This is likely to
remain true for many years to come.   The possession of
wealth is an insufficient determinant of power.   So are
personal characteristics or sheer activity in the sub-community.   And no particular stand on racial matters now
appears a sufficient basis in itself for power in the Crescent
sub-community.   Rather, a combination of these factors
is vitally important for today's leaders.   The position of the
Negro is undergoing a continuous process of change.   What
we are attempting to understand is not a static phenomenon.   Any model of power in the sub-community must be
dynamic.

6. Myrdal, *An American Dilemma*, II, 720-80.

CHAPTER VIII

THE EMERGING BIRACIAL
STRUCTURE OF POWER

IN this study we have examined minority power and race relations in Crescent City in the period following the Supreme Court decision of 1954. Some of the conclusions that proceed from our study have ramifications for the study of community-centered power and race relations everywhere.

Investigations of community power have been handicapped by lack of tools suitable for the observation, measurement, and analysis of different distributions of power. Apparently, none of the critics of the methodology used in power studies to date has discovered a procedure which, by itself, is any more reliable for ferreting out the power leaders of a given community. Perhaps social science in its present state does not have methods which can satisfactorily demonstrate the existence of power. I do hope, however, that studies such as this one, which utilize a variety of checks and balances, may perhaps offer as much reliability as the present state of the science allows.

The Spearman rank correlation derived from power-attribution selections of the sub-community sample and the Negro leader poll revealed a significant association between the two. This association sharply contradicts those who believe that power is wielded behind the scenes by "insiders." My study suggests that lines of communication are open between Negro community leaders and their followers.   Additional research on community power might well disclose that the general citizen is more sensitive to the community power structure than some studies have conceded.[1]

The significant agreement between the power attribution rankings by Negro and white informants in Crescent City demonstrated by the Kendall coefficient of concordance represents a definite difference from other research findings and serves to underline the essential uniqueness of any given community.   Although I had thought that lines of communication and interaction in Crescent would not be as attenuated as they were in some other cities studied, I did not anticipate as much mutual perception as I actually found.   In spite of tensions created by the Supreme Court decision, communication continues, and the liberal Negro leader has gained access to the white power structure on both formal and informal bases.

My investigation showed, moreover, a significant relationship between the top 31 power nominees and the active decision-makers.   This relationship is evidence in opposition to some of the postulates of critics of the power-attribution method.[2]   Approximately 71 per cent of the

1. Recent studies that have raised questions about "behind-the-scenes" power include Robert O. Schulze and Leonard U. Blumberg, "The Determination of Local Power Elites," *American Journal of Sociology,* LXIII (November, 1957), 290-96; Nelson W. Polsby, "Three Problems in the Analysis of Community Power," *American Sociological Review,* 24 (December, 1959), 796-803.   For studies that suggest that community power operates covertly, see C. Wright Mills, "The Middle Class in Middle-Sized Cities," *American Sociological Review,* 13 (December, 1946), 520-29; Floyd Hunter, *Community Power Structure* (Chapel Hill: University of North Carolina Press, 1953); Robert S. Lynd and Helen M. Lynd, *Middletown in Transition* (New York: Harcourt, Brace and Company, 1937), pp. 38-39, 97; W. Lloyd Warner *et al., Democracy in Jonesville* (New York: Harper and Brothers, 1949), pp. 100-3.

2. Representative of the current critics is Raymond E. Wolfinger, "Reputation and Reality in the Study of 'Community Power,'" *American Sociological Review,* 25 (October, 1960), 636-44.   Many valid criticisms have been made of the power-attribution method.   But implicit in Wolfinger's critique, as in the work of other recent critics, are two

power nominees were active in the issues scrutinized. By using both approaches—power attribution and decision-making—I avoided the possibility of selecting leaders active only in specific controversies. I was able to discern that certain individuals had more power than their sociometric ratings alone would have allowed them. Progressive shifts in the leadership structure were uncovered; the role of the race leader in today's power structure was disclosed.

I did not develop a systematic theory of minority power. Structures of power are often dependent upon local conditions. History, immediate traditions, and specific institutional and social characteristics appear to mold the form of power structures. Crescent City's sub-community is evidence of the importance of local variation. Students of power phenomena have frequently slighted individual community variations in their attempt to construct *the* model of power, and current models are inadequate for many situations as a result.

Several models of community power are discussed rather commonly in the literature. In the multi-purpose or interlocking power structure, power leaders are drawn largely from the economic dominants of the community. They agree on basic policies; they register their preferences on all major decisions. They constitute a relatively stable group and exhibit family continuity over several genera-

---

doubtful premises: first, that power in the community can or should be equated with *political* power in the community; and second, that power will always vary from issue to issue, with a specialized leadership model of power being the accurate model of community power. His desire to abandon completely the power-attribution approach is, therefore, questionable. (See Harry M. Scoble, "Yankeetown: Leadership in Three Decision Making Processes" [Paper presented at a meeting of the American Political Science Association, Washington, D.C., 1956]. Scoble, using both an index of leadership activity and the power-attribution method, found, contrary to Wolfinger, Polsby and others, that the latter was a more meaningful method for discerning power of specialized leaders in basic community issues.)

tions. The spheres-of-influence or polynucleated structure is composed of specialized leadership cliques which exert influence over the various areas of decision-making. One group may operate on the political level, another on the economic level, a third on the educational level—with little overlap. The coalition model, in essence, is a combination of the first two types. Specialized areas of activity in the understructure of community power are recognized, but a nucleus of individuals (usually economic or political dominants) whose role is to co-ordinate and approve strategies in all areas of community endeavor is also regarded as being present.

The present study does not support any single model of power, for to do so would be to ignore the power potential of other organized minority groupings, the influence of articulate citizens, and the very real problems associated with biracial community power. In fact, the power structure of Crescent City's minority community resembles in some ways each of the three models; it also is in some ways strikingly different from them.

Crescent City's is a composite power structure consisting of representatives from financial, professional, and commercial circles. Power leaders operate through organizations when decisions are made, but they are a fluid group which is altered as new men assume positions of organizational influence and as patterns of race relations shift. Yet continuity and stability are supplied by the old families and the strong institutions and organizations which have provided and continue to provide numbers of leaders at all levels.

Power leaders are a fairly cohesive group and are similar to one another in education, in degree of community participation, in the nature of their political and civic activities, and in their point of view toward Negro protest and civil rights. They nevertheless have their differences.

Much of the literature led me to expect that the economic elite would monopolize the power picture. It came as something of a surprise, therefore, to find the professionals and smaller businessmen playing an active role. Furthermore, the leaders were almost equally distributed among the upper and middle classes. Top positions of power were held by economic dominants, but as a group they did not monopolize positions of power. Within the minority community, 33 men were considered to be economic dominants by virtue of their key positions in the major firms of the city. Yet of this number, only 39 per cent were among the 31 power nominees and only 30 per cent were active power leaders in the basic community issues. The strong representation of the professionals—ministers, lawyers, and college faculty and administration—reflects the stability of the Negro social structure. Such professionals have long been part of the power structure of the city. It is clear that capable members of the middle class have more opportunity to increase their power as education improves and as community issues are regarded more and more as racial issues.

I was able to identify a corps of leaders who remained much the same from issue to issue. I was also able to identify lesser leaders who were active only in specific situations. My study did disclose dissension among the power leaders over the means of achieving their goals, but despite this conflict it found power leaders to be united by their efforts to present a solid front to the white community. The astute maneuvers and compromises that take place within the power structure have allowed Negro leaders to reach a consensus on most basic issues and to move with some assurance toward community goals. Contrary to some findings, I think it is proper to conclude that bargaining is a necessary part of the community power picture and that so-called hierarchies of power have little ultimate meaning.

Power leaders legitimize their actions by working through influential voluntary associations in establishing strategy and policy. Though these organizations play a vital part in the structure of sub-community power, some students have given only passing attention to the fact that top leaders rely on their influence.[3] Others have maintained that the role of organizations is in the execution of policy rather than in its formulation.[4] More research is needed, but I suspect that the power struggle is more often fought at the organizational level than at the individual level and that organizations play a significant role in policy formulation and decision-making.

Through the basic organizations and various institutions, lesser leaders and articulate citizens gain access to decision-making and the decision-makers. The power process in Crescent City is not closed, as it seems to be in some other communities studied. From the apex of community leadership and organization, specific policies are executed in a radiating process involving the other leaders and associations of the sub-community. Gradually the full resources of the minority group are brought into play.

There are a number of similarities between white and Negro community structures in Crescent City. There is, in fact, the possibility that the future may find the majority and minority structures fusing, so that the separate identity of the two is blurred. It is doubtful that these similarities in structure of the majority-minority group exist in less

3. See, for example, Delbert C. Miller, "Industry and Community Power Structure: A Comparative Study of an American and an English City," *American Sociological Review*, 23 (February, 1958), 13.
4. Floyd Hunter, *Community Power Structure* (Chapel Hill: University of North Carolina Press, 1953), p. 82; Roland J. Pellegrin and Charles H. Coates, "Absentee-Owned Corporations and Community Power Structure," *The American Journal of Sociology*, LXI (March, 1956), 413-19.

stable Negro communities—the literature itself discloses this.[5] The degree of integration in the broader community, size of population, type of socio-economic base, amount of political participation, number of articulate citizens, and type of race leaders all influence the nature of the power groupings present. Comparative research on minority power structures may reveal that more fluid and unstable models represent typical minority patterns.

Community power studies seem, it is clear, to be moving toward a typology of power structures as a mode of analysis. Contingent upon peculiar conditions and processes, power undoubtedly is geared to operate differently within diverse communities. But we may find that it is not possible to state generalizations about power structure that will apply across community lines. Should future research prove the typology to be a useful means for dealing with community power, however, it is likely that power-structure typologies will tend to be different for minority than for majority communities.

My analysis of community issues clearly revealed that the leaders most active in the school integration battle played the major role in the various political, economic, and civic issues before the community. Since 1954 the sub-community's bid for greater participation in all phases of community life was projected into a wide range of areas. The struggle against segregation shifted from the narrower confines of the legal arena to the broad sphere of community organization. All issues now bear on desegregation. As I have noted, the ability of minority leaders to raise Crescent City issues to the level of controversy has become a real source of power.

5. See, for example, Lewis Killian and Charles U. Smith, "Negro Protest Leaders in a Southern Community," *Social Forces,* 38 (March, 1960), 253-57, and Ernest A. T. Barth and Baha Abu-Laban, "Power Structure and the Negro Sub-Community," *American Sociological Review,* 24 (February, 1959), 74-76; James Q. Wilson, *Negro Politics: The Search for Leadership* (Glencoe, Ill.: The Free Press, 1960).

The Negro leaders are continually pressing, with real hope of success, for serious readjustments in Crescent City's power structure. They broke the segregated school pattern with litigation but without the actual legal coercion of a court order. They obtained a decisive voice in the policies and decisions relating to a state-wide project for industrial and economic expansion. They proved instrumental in defeating reactionary anti-Negro forces who tried to gain control of city-county government in 1957. By swinging their support to the more moderate white leaders, they obtained representation on the City Council, the school board, the Urban Renewal Board, the Economic and Development Board, the fire department, the police department, and the county sheriff's office. They persuaded the city to adopt a more liberal policy in the use of various community facilities—recreation areas, buses, ball parks. These and many other actions illustrate the success of the Negro bid for community power.

One must not of course infer that Negroes have achieved unlimited success. Many areas of community life are still blocked to them, and many of their attempts to alter segregated patterns have failed. Recently, for example, an attempt to defeat a bond issue for new educational facilities until more complete school integration was practiced met with failure. The white forces rallied support for the issue through a successful educational program, and the denial of support was not a popular policy within the sub-community itself in the first place. Leaders were somewhat divided, and the Negro community revealed a corresponding lack of accord. The Negro vote on the education bond issue, although it reflected the official position of the sub-community, was not decisive, and this failure prompted a return to the courts for relief. Following the bond vote, a new case was filed in which 161 additional children sought entrance into predominantly white schools.

The minority leaders generally work with the solid approval of the sub-community on desegregation issues. Support through bloc voting has been important in helping the Negro leaders to gain a voice in the biracial community. The Negro public has also upheld its leaders in their attempts to break segregated school patterns. Between 1957 and 1960, over 300 families came forward to submit mass reassignment requests intended to force the admission of Negro children into white schools. Probably in no other city in the South has the Negro leadership been more successful in gaining the backing of the Negro citizenry on this issue.

Interviews in the sub-community revealed strong support for the top leaders. Some 63.4 per cent of the sample favored desegregation of schools and other facilities. Only 8.6 per cent expressed opposition. Approximately 61 per cent agreed with the actions of the leaders on the issues, and only 7.8 per cent were in disagreement. All classes gave this support, but attitudes varied by social class. The higher the class of the respondents, the more likely they were to be in accord with their leaders. Leaders, then, draw most of their support from articulate upper- and middle-class followers.[6]

Negro leaders, like everyone else, were found to participate in established patterns of interaction within definable groups. Just as they have influenced their followers, so the sub-community has exerted influence over them. It

6. The nature of the interview data obtained from the sub-community has raised some questions about data analysis. Conclusions drawn about lower-class respondents, especially, have been obscured by the high "no response" received on certain questions. The problems encountered in the interviewing situation raise a number of important problems which need further research in terms of class-caste bias. For example, would Negro interviewers obtain more accurate data and fewer "no responses" than white interviewers? What different kinds of bias might a Negro interviewer inject into the data? These and many similar problems merit further study by those involved in minority research.

has shaped their attitudes, their values, and their desires. The leaders therefore evidence a measure of conformity to the norms of the Negro community—especially on the basis of class affiliation—in terms of the aspirations and desires of minority people.   Too, they have been influenced by the sentiments and values of the larger white community. This influence has been described by many students and needs no special comment here.   It should be noted, however, that the slowly changing patterns of American society have tended to transform the attitudes and values of Crescent City's Negro leadership into new patterns.   It should also be noted that, through its leaders, the Negro community has been successful in exerting influence over the white community by imposing certain claims upon it.

The Negroes of Crescent City have recently achieved a measure of political power as a result of direct federal protection of lawful franchise.   While not always successful, political bargaining has become an extremely important process for influencing the larger community. The 1954 Supreme Court decision broke the vicious circle that had trapped the Negro in an inferior position.   It gave legitimacy to his desire for equal rights.   It gave him self-respect, moral support, and an increasing desire to obtain complete realignment of his position in American life.

The white community at large and the white leaders find their position challenged—legally and ethically.   The changing relation between Negroes and whites involves conflict, but cannot be expressed simply in terms of contention between groups for a limited amount of power within the community.   Rather, it represents an attempt to create new power—to expand the power structure so that the total community population will be meaningfully represented in community life.   Minority leaders are now mobilizing the resources of their community for the attainment of goals to which a general commitment has already been made within our society.   What has occurred in Crescent City can be expected to occur in other communities as Negroes make additional gains in their bid for a strategic place in the community power structure.

APPENDIX A, APPENDIX B, BIBLIOGRAPHY,
AND INDEX

APPENDIX A

GLOSSARY

For the purposes of this study, certain working definitions growing out of related literature, theory, and practice were used. Many of the concepts are common to sociological writing; however, since different inflections of meaning can be attached to certain of them, I think it is advisable to specify the principal terms and how they are used.

ASSOCIATION: A group organized for pursuit of some common interest or group of interests in the community. An organization within the community.[1] Used interchangeably with *community organization.*

COMMUNICATION: A process of interaction in which ideas, sentiments, and beliefs are exchanged or shared through transmission.

COMMUNITY: A functionally related aggregate of people interacting within a specific geographic locality over time, structurally arranged, and exhibiting some awareness of their identity as a group.[2]

Sub-Community: A functional sub-system found within a larger community aggregate, with organized ways, structure, and patterns of behavior that are distinct from, and yet a part of and influenced by, the larger whole.

1. Robert M. MacIver, *Society* (New York: Farrar and Rinehart, 1937), p. 11.

2. Adapted from August B. Hollingshead, "Community Research: Development and Present Conditions," *American Sociological Review,* 13 (April, 1948), 136-48; Blaine E. Mercer, *The American Community* (New York: Random House, 1956), p. 25; and George A. Hillery, Jr., "Definitions of Community: Areas of Agreement," *Rural Sociology,* 20 (June, 1955), 111-23.

The term will be employed to designate the Negro community within the larger biracial setting and will be used synonymously with *Negro community*.

DECISION: A choice among alternative modes of action made by individuals or groups that involves action toward change or maintenance of community life or facilities.[3]

While several students have indicated that leaders are those individuals with relatively great influence over decisions, some see *power* as the actual participation in the making of decisions.[4] Thus, the persons of power status become the leaders most likely to be *decision-makers* within the community. I am not implying that members of a given power structure are the only decision-makers. I am simply saying that those who have power have, by virtue of their key position in the leadership structure, more opportunity to make and affect decisions. *Decision-making* is one result of power status.

INFLUENCE: Cf. *Power*.

INSTITUTION: A stable and organized system of behavior developed within a given society to serve certain needs or social objectives regarded as essential for the survival of the group. The main concern in this study is with the familial, religious, economic, political, and educational institutions.[5]

INTERACTION: A process by which individuals or groups exert influence upon one another. A reciprocal relationship is implied.

LEADER: An individual whose behavior affects the patterning of behavior within the community at a given time.[6]

General Leadership Structure: All those individuals in the sub-community who were found to be playing a leader-

3. Peter H. Rossi, "Community Decision Making," *Administrative Science Quarterly,* 1 (March, 1957), 415.

4. Harold D. Lasswell and Abraham Kaplan, *Power and Society* (New Haven: Yale University Press, 1950), pp. 74-75.

5. Adapted from George A. Lundberg, C. C. Schrag, and O. N. Larsen, *Sociology* (Rev. ed.; New York: Harper and Brothers, 1958), p. 757.

6. See E. S. Bogardus, *Leaders and Leadership* (New York: D. Appleton-Century Co., 1934), p. 3; A. W. Gouldner, *Studies in Leadership* (New York: Harper and Brothers, 1950), p. 20; Gardner Lindzey (ed.), *Handbook of Social Psychology* (Cambridge, Mass.: Addison-Wesley Publishing Co., 1954), II, 877-917.

ship role at some level of community organization. Included are power nominees, power leaders, and lesser leaders perceived to be active and subsequently observed to be active in various issues or problems throughout the sub-community.

Power Nominees: Those individuals who were *perceived* to have power and influence or were reputed to be the most influential decision-makers by three groups of informants—Negro leaders, white leaders, and the Negro-community sample. They are also referred to as the *top 31 leaders*—those who by their sociometric ratings appeared on the list of 31 perceived power leaders.

Top Power and Sub-Power Nominees: Occasionally, for purposes of data analysis this general group of power nominees was broken down into two sub-groups—*top power nominees* and *sub-power nominees.* The top power nominees are the ten individuals who received the largest number of nominations as power leaders. The sub-power nominees are the individuals who appear on the list of 31 power nominees but whose sociometric rating places them in the lower limits of the sociometric scale. This distinction is made in chapter IV particularly. Unless otherwise specified throughout the rest of the study, the term *power nominees* includes the sub-group as well.

Lesser Leaders: Individuals who appeared as community leaders in the leadership study but were not considered power leaders or decision-makers by their peers and whose actions on community issues place them outside the power-leader group. They make up the *sub-structure of community leadership.*

Power Leaders: Those among the power nominees who were found to be playing the most active role in community issues and decision-making. They are the *decision-makers* operating in a more or less generalized area of activity. The power leadership is made up of both power and sub-power nominees who were found to be operating at the policy and decision levels.

There are those who have taken issue with the coupling of "power" and "leader" into a single descriptive term.[7]   It would seem, however, that this term, like similar terms used in the literature—"power holder," "power wielder," "power figure"—is simply a descriptive tool that enables the researcher to distinguish among the different levels at which community leadership is seen to operate.   If we accept as a basic premise that communities and societies have some kind of power aggregate, then we must have some way to distinguish among those individuals within it.   Power leader is the term I find convenient.

Economic Dominants: Those individuals who hold top executive positions in one of the large banking, financial, or insurance firms and who are members of the governing board of one or more of these firms.   Persons in this group may or may not be part of the leadership and power structure of the sub-community.

Positional Leaders: Ex-officio or prestige leaders who can be identified as leaders by virtue of some office held. They may or may not be power nominees or power leaders.

OFFICE: Cf. *Position.*

ORGANIZATION: The process of co-ordinating activities so that the parts become interdependent and the system functions as a unit.

POSITION: The individual's place in a given social system.   Following Davis, I consider *status* and *office* to be two kinds of position.

Status: A type of position which is recognized in a given social system and is spontaneously evolved.

Office: A position which is deliberately created and governed by specific rules.[8]

POWER: The ability to induce people to take courses of action they might not otherwise have taken.

Influence: Influence and *power* are concepts used to describe relationships between individuals and groups.   When we say an individual or group is influential or powerful

7. See Edward C. Banfield, "The Concept of Leadership in Community Research" (Paper presented at a meeting of the American Political Science Association, St. Louis, Mo., 1958).

8. Adapted from Kingsley Davis, *Human Society* (New York: The Macmillan Co., 1948), pp. 85-89.

we mean that his or its behavior has significance for some other individual or group. Influence is often defined as the ability to affect the behavior or policies of another. However, in the case of influence, the literature stresses that it is submitted to voluntarily. Power then becomes a special case of the exercise of influence in general. Following this notion is Barber's contention that power is illegitimate influence and authority is legitimate influence.[9] The implicit possibility of sanctions becomes the basic distinction between power and influence. But this distinction is difficult to deal with empirically. One man's legitimate influence may be another's illegitimate influence. And authority has a tendency to slide over into power without one's being able to distinguish the point of alteration. Too, the average informant tends to use the words as equivalent. But more important, it is difficult for the researcher to be absolutely certain when B is responding to A because he fears some possible sanction—e.g. ridicule, loss of job or office, of status, of prestige, or physical injury, etc.—and when he is responding voluntarily to advice because he admires, respects, agrees with, aspires to be like, or identifies with A. Further, B may feel that there are possible sanctions when none can actually be called into existence. Or B may consciously feel that he is simply being influenced or seeking advice voluntarily when sub-consciously he fears sanctions.

Thus, although in each case the process by which A affects B—by power or influence—may be different, the general form of the relationship is the same. And researches of power and influence tend to follow the same basic designs. Significant conceptual differences are recognized as being important, but my experience in the research situation indicates that it is advisable to use the two concepts as being roughly synonymous. A

9. Bernard Barber, *Social Stratification* (New York: Harcourt, Brace and Co., 1957), pp. 232-63. The distinction between legitimate power, or authority, and illegitimate power is well defined in the literature. See, for example, Rupert B. Vance, "Freedom and Authority in the Social Structure," in *Freedom and Authority in Our Time,* ed. Lyman Bryson *et al.* (New York: Harper and Brothers, 1953), pp. 350-54.

similar conclusion has been reached by a number of other students of power and influence.[10]

POWER PROCESS: The more dynamic aspects of power; power in action. The power process is the focus on decision-making and issues over time.

POWER STRUCTURE: Those leaders and those parts of the community institutional and associational structure which may come into play as a result of various community issues or decisions.[11]

RACE LEADER: From the pilot study in Crescent City a fourfold classification (based on self-identification as well as peer-group identification) evolved—radical, liberal, moderate, and conservative. As used in this work, therefore, "race leader" will be conceived of as the leader who, by his stand on certain issues, can be identified in terms of a radical, liberal, moderate, or conservative approach.

ROLE: The part played by the person in the group or social situation; the action of the individual leader in the community as dictated by his position.[12]

SOCIAL CLASS: Groups of individuals who, through similarity of such criteria as education, occupation, housing, and economic background, and through similarity of values, attitudes, and behavior, can be regarded as belonging to a given stratum of a community.

SOCIAL ORGANIZATION: Used here in an all-inclusive sense to embrace the totality of continuing social relationships which develop in a society. The complex structure of institutions, associations, and social relationships in their dynamic functioning and interplay.[13]

SOCIAL PROCESS: The characteristic way interaction occurs, or a series of related events leading to some result.

SOCIAL STRUCTURE: Relatively fixed, persistent, and functional-

10. See, for example, work by Hunter, Scoble, Agger, Schulze, Blumberg, Simons, and Dahl.

11. Delbert C. Miller, "Industry and Community Power Structure: A Comparative Study of an American and an English City," *American Sociological Review*, 23 (February, 1958), 10.

12. Adapted from Ralph Linton, *Study of Man* (New York: D. Appleton-Century Co., 1936).

13. Gordon W. Blackwell, "A Theoretical Framework for Sociological Research in Community Organization," *Social Forces*, 33 (October, 1954), 57-58.

ly interrelated units or elements of a social group or social system, such as institutions, social classes, associations, leadership and power groupings, racial groups, and other enduring social units.

STATUS: Cf. *Position.*

SUB-COMMUNITY: Cf. *Community.*

APPENDIX B

WORKING HYPOTHESES

The following working hypotheses grew out of research and assumptions and theories in the literature relating to community power studies and southern Negro communities.

1. METHODOLOGY

Because of the institutional and organizational structure of the Crescent City sub-community:

    a. The findings of the two variations of the power attribution method used in the sub-community to identify Negro leadership and power would be significantly associated.

    b. The findings of the power-attribution method utilized among the white leaders would not demonstrate significant agreement with those findings from the sub-community polls.

    c. The findings of the case-study decision-making method for identifying functional leadership would vary slightly from the findings of the power-attribution methods.

2. POWER RELATIONS

    a. Within the sub-community social structure there was a power group the leadership role of which tended to be generalized.

        Corollary 1. The power leaders would be drawn from the dominant economic and professional institutions.

        Corollary 2. The power leaders would tend to operate within the framework of key civic, economic, social, and political associations.

> *Corollary 3.* Lesser community leaders would have access to power and power leaders through these associational groupings.

b. In order to present a "united front" to the white community, the general leadership structure would tend to *appear* monistic in its approach to community issues.

> *Corollary 1.* Consensus on basic issues would result only after considerable maneuvering and compromise on the part of power leaders and the sub-structure of community leadership.

c. Decisions of the sub-community power leaders tended to have increasingly important ramifications for Crescent City as a whole.

> *Corollary 1.* The Negro leader's access to power in the larger community would not have diminished but rather in some areas—particularly those allied to the desegregation of public and quasi-public institutions—would have tended to increase as a result of the 1954 Supreme Court decision.

3. PATTERNS OF COMMUNICATION AND INTERACTION

a. Communication and interaction between Negro leaders and their followers would tend toward openness but would vary by social class.

> *Corollary 1.* The perception and attitudes sub-community members held with regard to leaders and to issues such as desegregation would reflect this class variation. (1) The higher a sub-community member was on the social scale, the easier it became for him to identify the power leadership. (2) The higher a sub-community member was on the social scale, the greater were the chances of his being in accord with the actions and policies of the power leadership.
>
> *Corollary 2.* The general stand Negro power leaders took regarding various issues tended to

reflect the sentiments and desires of their motivated and articulate (upper- and middle-class) followers.

b. Formal and informal lines of communication and interaction between Negro leaders and white leaders, while partially blocked—especially with regard to desegregation—would be present and operative.

4. RACE LEADER ROLES AND DESEGREGATION

a. The role of Negro power leaders could not be separated from their race leader role.

> *Corollary 1.* Within the Negro leadership structure there was a diversity of race leader types that could be identified by attitudes or actions on desegregation.
>
> *Corollary 2.* The desegregation issue would result in a gain in influence and power for certain race leader types and a loss in influence and power for other race leader types.

METHODOLOGY

PRELIMINARY SOURCES OF DATA

The researcher used a variety of techniques in securing data for this study. Census reports, maps, Chamber of Commerce and community-development information, and city planning and public works data provided a basic background. Materials dealing with the history of the white and Negro community and data regarding early white and Negro leaders were secured. Community newspapers, both white and Negro, provided an additional and current source of data. Articles dealing with issues, organizations, and individuals pertinent to the study were clipped and catalogued over a three-year period.

COLLECTION OF POWER ATTRIBUTION DATA

Negro Leadership Poll Sample. As one approach to the study of Negro power relations in Crescent City, a variation of the chain-referral or snowball technique—based on the reputation of leaders among community members—was utilized. The methodology at this level called for interviewing four groups of individuals. The interview schedules were pre-tested in the winter and spring of 1957 and revised for use in the present study.

(1) The Experience Survey (unstructured). In order to begin the collection of data on Crescent City's Negro leadership, contacts were made with individuals of considerable experience in the field of investigation—"experts." Four individuals were interviewed to secure suggestions about the project, suggestions about key informant nominees, and suggestions about the best approach to key informants. Three "experts" were Negro; one was white. One was a political scientist, one an anthropologist, one a sociologist, and one a historian. They had from fifteen to twenty-five years of firsthand contact with the community. All were familiar with, and interested in, race and power relations.

They were asked to name those persons in the sub-community who, by virtue of their position in the community and knowledge about community affairs, could serve as key informants in a preliminary listing of the influential leaders. There was a striking similarity in the nominations made by the "experts." Three individuals received four votes, four received three, and five received two.

(2) Key Informant Interviews (semi-structured). The individuals whose names were obtained from interviews with the "experts" served as key informants for the next step in the design. Those individuals receiving two or more nominations were contacted and twelve men were interviewed in order to solicit information about leadership and community organizations. The men selected represented the basic institutions and organizations of the sub-community. Since most of the informants named by the experts had been nominated, in part at least, by virtue of positions held in the sub-community structure, all of them appeared at least once among the nominations made by the key informants themselves.

Each key informant was asked to name the fifteen top leaders in the community and the ten most influential community organizations. Relation to leaders named and membership in organizations mentioned were also asked, in order to discover possible biasing factors. From the interviews with the key informants, some seventy persons were identified as leaders, forty-two of these being nominated at least twice.

(3) Community Leader Interviews (semi-structured). The

forty-two nominees who had received two or more nominations
from key informants made up a basic list of leaders to be
interviewed. A semi-structured schedule was used to solicit
information germane to certain of the research hypotheses.
Identifying information—age, place of birth, years of residence
in Crescent City, religious affiliation, education, occupation,
kinds of property owned, and number of employees supervised
or directed—was obtained.

Each person was handed the basic list of leaders nominated
by key informants and asked to add other names to this list.
He was then asked to identify at least five top leaders in the
sub-community "from the point of view of their ability to make
decisions and to make or affect policy." He was quizzed about
leaders who had lost power as a result of the desegregation
issue. Information about types of race leaders was secured.

A series of questions was included to discover the amount
of communication and interaction among leaders, both Negro
and white. After listing what they considered to be the most
important or influential community organizations and associations, respondents were asked to give their membership in
organizations and the memberships they shared with the five
leaders named by them. A similar series of questions was included with regard to biracial and Negro committees, boards,
and projects on the local, state, and national levels.

A question on the respondents' role in desegregation activities and a discussion of the role of other leaders in the desegregation issue followed. Data relating to white attitudes
toward desegregation and the effect opposition to desegregation
had were obtained. Questions on major problems facing the
sub-community concluded the interview. The interview time
ranged from approximately one hour to two and one-half hours,
depending upon the interest and available time of informants.

Forty additional names were given to the investigator by
respondents. Of these, twelve received more than two mentions and were added to a final master list for interviewing
purposes. Of the final list of fifty-four subjects, forty-nine
completed interviews employing the Negro leader poll schedules. The investigator met for a short time with two others
who insisted they could not be of help and preferred not to
respond to any questions. One other subject failed to keep
four successive appointments, and two were unavailable for

interviewing purposes. From the responses of the forty-nine informants came the list of attributed power and sub-power nominees.

(4) Power Nominee Interviews (non-structured). Upon completion of the interviews of community leaders, those who appeared as the top power and sub-power nominees (that is, sociometric leaders most frequently selected by others) were reinterviewed in order to obtain further data concerning their patterns of interaction, their activities in desegregation and other community issues, and the entire decision-making process. Thirty repeat interviews were held with reputed top leaders. In six cases a third interview was held to gain additional information.

Sub-Community Sample Interview (structured). In order to obtain a stratified sample of the sub-community, Negro residential districts were mapped according to the class (upper, middle, and lower). This distinction was made in three ways. First, the writer, assisted by field workers, spent two weeks driving through Crescent City's Negro neighborhoods by automobile, rating blocks on the basis of external appearances, as suggested by Warner.[1] Each block in the Negro community was assigned a class on the basis of the observations. Rating of houses took into consideration such criteria as size and condition of house, state of repair, condition of grounds, nearness to adjacent building, aesthetic appeal, and architectural design. A six-point scale was used: very good–good, upper class; average–fair, middle class; poor–very poor, lower class. The dwelling areas were rated in a similar manner, according to the over-all appearance of the neighborhood, as high, above average, average, below average, low and very low.[2]

Second, the writer checked Crescent City Planning Office studies, tax-assessment maps, residential zoning maps, and other such analyses in order to determine possible discrepancies in the observational mapping. Third, the senior Negro member of the Crescent City Welfare Department was consulted, and the Negro community was mapped by class areas according to departmental criteria. This map was used as a final check before the stratified Negro community map to be used for the purposes of this study was drawn.

1. Lloyd Warner *et al., Social Class in America* (Chicago: Science Research Associates, 1949), pp. 143-54.
2. *Ibid.,* p. 154.

Though rating was made on the basis of individual houses as well as of total dwelling areas, I was of course concerned with blocks rather than single dwelling units or entire neighborhoods. Block classes were arrived at by combining the scores of the majority of dwelling units in the block with the dwelling-area score. A second appraisal of housing types was made by interviewers and served as one criteria for determining individual community members' position in the social-class scale.

Sample blocks were drawn from each "residential class area." Blocks were numbered, and block numbers were selected from a table of random numbers. Of the 283 interview schedules which were completed, 85 were upper class, 100 were middle class, and 98 were lower class.

Starting at the second house from the northern right hand corner and working counterclockwise on each block selected, field workers interviewed respondents in every third house. Apartments were considered as separate units. If no one responded, a second call was made, and if this second attempt failed, an adjoining unit was visited. Refusals were treated as "no responses."

In the schedule used in the community sample, identifying information was asked about age, sex, years of residence in Crescent City, place of birth, religious affiliation, number of children, occupation, present employment status, and education. From data obtained in the pilot study and from leads gleaned from newspaper data, a list of ten problems facing the sub-community was drawn up. These included (1) better housing facilities; (2) financial security and job opportunities; (3) better facilities and academic standards in the sub-community schools; (4) more and better recreational facilities; (5) desegregation in the schools; (6) desegregation of other local facilities— parks, busses, libraries, restaurants, churches, golf courses, etc.; (7) better communication with the white community; (8) more community spirit and participation in community affairs; (9) more political participation; and (10) better health and medical facilities. These problems were listed on cards and handed to respondents (or read to informant if educational background plus other subjective clues implied difficulty in comprehending material as written). The respondents were asked to add other problems that they felt should be included on the list. Items in the list were not mutually exclusive.

Some items were included in order to determine, if possible, attitudes on desegregation.

Questions were also asked that were designed to elicit a community member's perception of the most important problems facing the community and to determine what, if any, leaders were thought to be associated with specific problems. Respondents were requested to list the most influential leaders in the community and to explain their relationships, if any, with the leaders named. A question was included to determine awareness within the community of the organizations most functionally useful to the power leadership. Memberships held in these associations were noted by respondents. Two final questions were asked that specifically concerned informants' attitudes toward desegregation. A scale was constructed to determine how strongly the interviewee agreed or disagreed with the actions of the Negro community leaders on the issue.

White Community Leader Sample Interviews (semi-structured). In order to determine how the Crescent City Negro leadership was perceived by white community leaders and to gain information about their attitudes and actions on community issues, a sample of Crescent City's white leadership was interviewed. Although a list of the top white power leaders was available from previous studies conducted in the urban Middle South, the author chose to select a leader at random and to work out separately by the "snowball" method the networks of claimed power and influence. (This approach served as a reliable check, as I noted in chapters IV and VI.) A schedule of open-end questions was constructed. These included queries about the respondents' personal data.

Informants were asked whom they regarded as the top Negro leaders. Questions intended to identify those Negro leaders considered to be "safe or accommodating" as opposed to those considered "unsafe or radical" were also included. Respondents were queried about formal and informal communication between whites and Negroes, about white leaders Negroes were most likely to consult on various issues, and about the effectiveness of Negro leaders in making their desires known and in obtaining positive action on the issues with which they were concerned.

Turning to the white leadership, itself, respondents indicated those persons they believed to be the most powerful white leaders from the standpoint of their ability to make decisions. and affect policy.

A final series of questions was directed toward school desegregation. The writer asked for attitudes on the issue and also inquired what leaders or organizations were most active in opposition to desegregation and what leaders or organizations were in favor of some form of desegregation. Inquiry was also made about the respondents' opininon of the differences between Crescent City and other Piedmont cities where some token integration had taken place without litigation. Finally the informants were questioned about their knowledge of the whole issue—possible and actual litigation procedures, the record of decisions made by both whites and Negroes regarding the issue, and the respondents' own role, if any, in the problem.

Twenty interviews were held. All but two of the respondents with whom the researcher talked appeared on the list of "top leaders" obtained from the southern urban study project. Of these, about three-fifths were among the power nominees, and the others were sub-power nominees. The two respondents who did not appear on the urban studies list were listed consistently by this writer's informants. One, a well-known attorney, appeared to be playing a key role in the white community's stalling action on desegregation and apparently wielded considerable influence in educational and political circles. The other individual had considerable influence in civic and religious affairs and was very active in the field of race relations.

Thirty persons were listed at least once by white leaders as Negro power leaders. Six of these persons received the majority of votes. Six did not appear in the Negro community surveys.

COLLECTION OF DATA ON ISSUES AND DECISIONS

In addition to the use of a battery of power attribution schedules, the researcher also attempted to observe, trace, or reconstruct the policies that had actually been formulated and the decisions that had actually been made on selected issues.

The issues which the researcher attempted to trace were (1) the establishment of the Mayor's Commission on Race Relations; (2) the development of a new Crescent City Industrial Education Center; (3) double sessions at Negro elementary schools and subsequent plans for reopening a con-

demned white school for use of Negro elementary students;
(4) selection and support of Negro and white candidates for
the City Council; and (5) litigation and mass reassignment
procedures for desegregation of Crescent City white schools.
In addition, brief mention was made of other issues that arose
during the period of field observation.

The first three issues mentioned have reached settlement
at this writing. The fourth issue extends over a five-year
period, and therefore provides an extended opportunity of observing how desegregation and its ramifications have affected
the status of certain Negro community leaders. In addition,
it indicates how political maneuvering plays an important part
in some of the power leaders' actions. The fifth issue has resulted in the admission of some Negro youths to white schools
but, as a result of the laws of Mid-South State, is likely to remain live in Crescent City for the next few years.

Data about issues and decisions were secured from the
following sources: personal observation of committee and organizational meetings related to the issues involved; special
documents, minutes of meetings, special committee and organizational reports, speeches, and policy statements; interview
materials, including appropriate elements of Negro and white
leadership interview schedules, special interviews with power
nominees and power leaders, and interviews with others who
were not part of the top leadership structure but who were
implicated in desegregation and related issues; and newspaper
files extending over a three-year period.

DATA COLLECTED THROUGH COMMUNITY FIELD OBSERVATION

Over a two-and-one-half-year period, the writer observed
the actions and attitudes of members of the sub-community,
especially the leaders, through participation in a variety of
community activities: church services, college and other educational functions, meetings of the Crescent Negro Council,
P.T.A. and other organizational groupings, and special community functions such as the dedication of recreation centers
and fire departments. The writer therefore had the opportunity to observe first-hand the patterns of interaction and influence, and this opportunity helped immeasurably to clarify
the questions about the roles of the various power figures in
the Crescent sub-community.

BIBLIOGRAPHY

Books

Barber, Bernard. *Social Stratification.* New York: Harcourt, Brace and Co., 1957.

Bendix, R., and S. M. Lipset. *Class, Status and Power.* Glencoe, Ill.: The Free Press, 1953.

Bennett, John and Melvin Tumin. *Social Life.* New York: Alfred A. Knopf, 1949.

Bogardus, Emory S. *Leaders and Leadership.* New York: D. Appleton-Century Co., 1934.

Chapin, F. Stuart. *The Impact of War on Community Leadership and Opinion in Red Wing.* Minneapolis: University of Minnesota Press, 1945.

Cox, Oliver. "Leadership Among Negroes in the United States," in *Studies in Leadership,* ed. A. W. Gouldner. New York: Harper and Brothers, 1950.

Dahl, Robert. "Hierarchy, Democracy and Bargaining in Politics and Economics," in *Research Frontiers in Politics and Government.* Washington, D. C.: Brookings Institution, 1955.

Davis, Kingsley. *Human Society.* New York: The Macmillan Co., 1948.

Dean, John, and Alex Rosen. *A Manual of Intergroup Relations.* Chicago: University of Chicago Press, 1955.

De Gré, Gerard. "Freedom and Social Structure," in *Sociological Analysis,* ed. Logan Wilson and William Kolb. New York: Harcourt, Brace and Co., 1949.

Drake, St. Clair, and H. R. Cayton. *Black Metropolis.* New York: Harcourt, Brace and Co., 1945.

Frazier, E. Franklin. *Black Bourgeoisie.* Glencoe, Ill.: The Free Press, 1957.

————. *The Negro in the United States.* New York: The Macmillan Co., 1949.

Gouldner, A. W. (ed.). *Studies in Leadership.* New York: Harper and Brothers, 1950.

Hunter, Floyd. *Community Power Structure.* Chapel Hill: University of North Carolina Press, 1953.

————. *Top Leadership, U.S.A.* Chapel Hill: University of North Carolina Press, 1959.

Jahoda, Marie, Morton Deutsch, and Stuart W. Cook. *Research Methods in Social Relations.* Part I. New York: The Dryden Press, 1951.

Kendall, M. G. *Rank Correlation Methods.* London: Griffin, 1948.

Key, V. O. *Southern Politics in State and Nation.* New York: Alfred A. Knopf, 1950.

Lasswell, Harold D., and Abraham Kaplan. *Power and Society.* New Haven: Yale University Press, 1950.

Latham, Earl. *The Group Basis of Politics.* Ithaca, N. Y.: Cornell University Press, 1952.

Lewis, Hylan. *Blackways of Kent.* Chapel Hill: University of North Carolina Press, 1953.

Lindzey, Gardner (ed.). *Handbook of Social Psychology.* 2 vols. Cambridge, Mass.: Addison-Wesley Publishing Company, 1954.

Lincoln, C. Eric. *The Black Muslins in America.* Boston: Beacon Press, 1961.

Linton, Ralph. *Study of Man.* New York: D. Appleton-Century Co., 1936.

Lipset, Seymour M. "Political Sociology," in *Sociology Today,* ed. R. K. Merton, L. Broom, and L. S. Cottrell, Jr. New York: Basic Books, Inc., 1959.

Lundberg, George A., C. C. Schrag, and O. N. Larsen. *Sociology.* Rev. ed. New York: Harper and Brothers, 1958.

Lynd, Robert S. "Power in American Society as Resource and Problem," in *Problems of Power in American Democracy,* ed. Arthur Kornhauser. Detroit: Wayne State University Press, 1957.

Lynd, Robert S., and Helen M. Lynd. *Middletown in Transition.* New York: Harcourt, Brace and Company, 1937.

MacIver, Robert M. *Society.* New York: Farrer and Rinehart, 1937.

————. *Web of Government.* New York: The Macmillan Co., 1947.

Mercer, Blaine E. *The American Community.* New York: Random House, 1956.

Merton, Robert K. *Social Theory and Social Structure.* Glencoe, Ill.: The Free Press, 1949.

————. "Patterns of Influence," in *Communications Research,* ed. Paul F. Lazarsfeld and Frank N. Stanton. New York: Harper and Brothers, 1949.

Mills, C. Wright. *The Power Elite.* New York: Oxford University Press, 1956.

Myrdal, Gunnar. *An American Dilemma.* 2 vols. New York: Harper and Brothers, 1944.

Park, Robert, E. W. Burgess, and R. D. McKenzie. *The City.* Chicago: University of Chicago Press, 1925.

Parsons, Talcott. *Essays in Sociological Theory, Pure and Applied.* Glencoe, Ill.: The Free Press, 1945.

Reitzes, Dietrich C. *Negroes and Medicine.* Cambridge, Mass.: Harvard University Press, 1958.

Riesman, David. "Who Has the Power?" in *Class, Status and Power,* ed. R. Bendix and S. M. Lipset. Glencoe, Ill.: The Free Press, 1953.

Rogers, Alan. "Some Aspects of Industrial Diversification in the United States," in *Papers and Proceedings of the Regional Science Association.* Vol. I. State College: Pennsylvania State University, 1955.

Rohrer, J. H., and M. S. Edmonson. *The Eighth Generation.* New York: Harper and Brothers, 1959.

Ross, Murray G. *Community Organization.* New York: Harper and Brothers, 1955.

Schermerhorn, R. A. *These Our People.* Boston: D. C. Heath and Co., 1949.

Siegel, Sidney. *Nonparametric Statistics.* New York: McGraw-Hill Book Company, Inc., 1956.

Simon, Herbert A. *Administrative Behavior.* New York: The Macmillan Co., 1945.

————. *Models of Man.* New York: John P. Wiley and Sons, 1957.

Simpson, George E., and J. Milton Yinger. *Racial and Cultural Minorities.* Rev. ed. New York: Harper and Brothers, 1958.

————. "The Sociology of Race and Ethnic Relations," in *Sociology Today,* ed. R. K. Merton *et al.* New York: Basic Books, Inc., 1959.

Suchman, Edward, *et al. Desegregation: Some Propositions and Research Suggestions.* New York: Anti-Defamation League of B'nai B'rith, 1958.

Tawney, R. H. *Equality.* London: Allen and Unwin, Ltd., 1929.

Thomas, W. I. *Social Behavior and Personality: Contributions of W. I. Thomas to Theory and Social Research,* ed. E. H. Volkart. New York: Social Science Research Council, 1951.

Truman, David. *The Governmental Process.* New York: Alfred A. Knopf, 1955.

Tumin, Melvin M. *Desegregation: Resistance and Readiness.* Princeton, N. J.: Princeton University Press, 1958.

United States Bureau of the Census. *Seventeenth Census of the United States: 1950.* Vol. II. Washington, D. C.: U. S. Government Printing Office, 1952.

United States Census City and County Data Book. Washington, D. C.: U. S. Government Printing Office, 1956.

Vance, Rupert B. "Freedom and Authority in the Social Structure," in *Freedom and Authority in Our Time,* ed. Lyman Bryson *et al.* New York: Harper and Brothers, 1953.

Warner, W. Lloyd, B. H. Junker, and W. A. Adams. *Color and Human Nature.* Washington: American Council on Education, 1941.

Warner, W. Lloyd, and Paul S. Lunt. *The Social Life of a Modern Community.* New Haven: Yale University Press, 1941.

Warner, W. Lloyd *et al. Democracy in Jonesville.* New York: Harper and Brothers, 1949.

————. *Social Class in America.* Chicago: Science Research Associates, 1949.

Weber, Max. "Class, Status, Party," *From Max Weber: Essays in Sociology,* ed. C. Wright Mills. Translated by H. H. Garth. New York: Oxford University Press, 1946.

Williams, Robin M., Jr. *American Society.* New York: Alfred A. Knopf, 1956.

————. "Race and Cultural Relations," in *Review of Soci-*

ology, ed. J. P. Gittler. New York: John P. Wiley and Sons, 1957.

Wilson, James Q. *Negro Politics: The Search for Leadership.* Glencoe, Ill.: The Free Press, 1960.

Periodicals

Agger, Robert. "Power Attributions in the Local Community: Theoretical and Research Considerations," *Social Forces,* 34 (May, 1956), 322-31.

Barth, Ernest A. T., and Baha Abu-Laban. "Power Structure and the Negro Sub-Community," *American Sociological Review,* 24 (February, 1959), 69-76.

Barth, Ernest A. T., and S. D. Johnson. "Community Power and a Typology of Social Issues," *Social Forces,* 38 (October, 1959), 29-33.

Belknap, George, and Ralph Smuckler. "Political Power Relations in a Midwestern City," *Public Opinion Quarterly,* 20 (Spring, 1956), 73-81.

Bell, Daniel. "Power Elite Reconsidered," *American Journal of Sociology,* LXIV (November, 1958), 238-50.

Bendix, R., and S. Lipset. "Political Sociology," *Current Sociology,* 6:2 (1957), 79-98.

Bierstedt, Robert. "An Analysis of Social Power," *American Sociological Review,* 15 (December, 1950), 730-38.

Blackwell, Gordon W. "A Theoretical Framework for Sociological Research in Community Organization," *Social Forces,* 33 (October, 1954), 56-64.

Edwards, Vinson A. "Negro Leadership in Rural Georgia Communities," *Social Forces,* 21 (October, 1942), 90-93.

Fanelli, A. A. "A Typology of Community Leadership," *Social Forces,* 34 (May, 1956), 332-38.

Fleming, Harold C. "Resistance Movements and Racial Segregation," *The Annals,* 304 (March, 1956), 44-52.

Frazier, E. Franklin. "Race Contacts and the Social Structure," *American Sociological Review,* 14 (February, 1949), 1-11.

Freeman, Charles, and Selz C. Mayo. "Decision Makers in Rural Community Action," *Social Forces,* 35 (May, 1957), 319-22.

Haer, John L. "Social Stratification in Relation to Attitudes

Toward Sources of Power in a Community," *Social Forces,* 35 (December, 1956), 137-42.

Hillery, George A., Jr. "Definitions of Community: Areas of Agreement," *Rural Sociology,* 20 (June, 1955), 111-23.

Hollingshead, August B. "Community Research: Development and Present Conditions," *American Sociological Review,* 13 (April, 1948), 136-46.

Johnson, Guy B. "Negro Racial Movements and Leadership in the United States," *American Journal of Sociology,* XLIII (July, 1937), 57-71.

Johnson, Guy B., and Richard Simpson. "Integration: A Human Relations Problem," *Phi Delta Kappan,* 37 (May, 1956), 321-33.

Kaufman, Herbert, and Victor Jones. "The Mystery of Power," *Public Administrative Review,* 14 (Spring, 1954), 205-18.

Killian, Lewis, and Charles U. Smith. "Negro Protest Leaders in a Southern Community," *Social Forces,* 38 (March, 1960), 253-57.

King, Charles E. "The Process of Social Stratification Among an Urban Southern Minority Population," *Social Forces,* 31 (May, 1953), 352-55.

Lenski, Gerhard E., and John C. Leggett. "Caste, Class, and Deference in the Research Interview," *American Journal of Sociology,* LXV (March, 1960), 463-67.

Lewis, Hylan, and Mozell Hill. "Desegregation, Integration and the Negro Community," *The Annals,* 304 (March, 1956), 116-23.

Lohman, J. P., and D. C. Reitzes. "Note on Race Relations in Mass Society," *American Journal of Sociology,* LVIII (November, 1952), 242.

Marsh, James G. "An Introduction to the Theory and Measurement of Influences," *American Political Science Review,* 49 (June, 1955), 432-51.

Merton, Robert. Discussion of papers by Talcott Parsons. *American Sociological Review,* 13 (April, 1948), 165-68.

Miller, Delbert C. "Industry and Community Power Structure: A Comparative Study of an American and an English City," *American Sociological Review,* 23 (February, 1958), 9-15.

Mills, C. Wright. "The Middle Class in Middle-Sized Cities,"

American Sociological Review, 13 (December, 1946), 520-29.

Parenton, Vernon J., and Roland Pellegrin. "Social Structure and Leadership Factors in a Negro Community," *Phylon,* 18 (First Quarter, 1956), 74-78.

Parsons, Talcott. "The Distribution of Power in American Society," *World Politics,* 10 (October, 1957), 123-43.

Pellegrin, Roland, and Charles H. Coates. "Absentee-Owned Corporations and Community Power Structures," *American Journal of Sociology,* LXI (March, 1956), 413-19.

Pfouts, Ralph W. "Economic Interrelations Between Cities in the Piedmont," *Research Previews* (Institute for Research in Social Science, University of North Carolina), 6 (March, 1959).

Polsby, Nelson W. "The Sociology of Community Power: A Reassessment," *Social Forces,* 37 (March, 1959), 232-36.

————. "Three Problems of Community Power Analysis," *American Sociological Review,* 24 (December, 1959), 796-803.

Record, Wilson. "Negro Intellectuals and Negro Movements: Some Methodological Notes," *The Journal of Negro Education,* 24 (Spring, 1955), 106-12.

Rossi, Peter H. "Community Decision Making," *Administrative Science Quarterly,* 1 (March, 1957), 415-41.

Roucek, Joseph S. "Minority-Majority Relations in Their Power Aspects," *Phylon,* 17 (First Quarter, 1956), 25-30.

Ryan, Bryce. "Social and Ecological Patterns in Farm Leadership of Four Iowa Townships," *Research Bulletin, Agriculture Experiment Station, Iowa State College,* 306 (September, 1942).

Schulze, Robert O. "The Role of Economic Dominants in Community Power Structure," *American Sociological Review,* 23 (February, 1958), 3-9.

Schulze, Robert O., and Leonard U. Blumberg. "The Determination of Local Power Elites," *American Journal of Sociology,* LXIII (November, 1957), 290-96.

Smythe, Hugh. "Negro Masses and Leaders Characteristics: An Analysis of Current Trends," *Sociology and Social Research,* 35 (September-October, 1950), 31-37.

Smythe, Hugh H. "Changing Patterns in Negro Leadership," *Social Forces,* 29 (December, 1950), 191-97.

Stewart, Frank A. "A Sociometric Study of Influence in Southtown," *Sociometry,* 10 (February, 1947), 273-86.
Wolfinger, Raymond E. "Reputation and Reality in the Study of 'Community Power,'" *American Sociological Review,* 25 (October, 1960), 636-44.

Unpublished Materials

Banfield, Edward C. "The Concept of Leadership in Community Research." Paper presented at the meeting of the American Political Science Association, St. Louis, Mo., 1958.
Denton, A. M. "Organization in a Depressed Community: A Study of Crisis and Leadership." Unpublished Master's thesis, University of North Carolina, 1951.
Scoble, Harry M. "Yankeetown: Leadership in Three Decision Making Processes." Paper presented at a meeting of the American Political Science Association, Washington, D. C., 1956.

INDEX

Accommodative leadership, 48, 149, 179-81, 206; loss of influence and power, 166, 181. *See also* Leader, Race leader

Associations, Negro, 33, 42, 47-48, 58, 60-61, 72-74; biracial participation in, 74, 110, 163, 164-65; as communication channels, 155, 163; white associations favoring desegregation, 172; definition of, 201. *See also* Communication, Organizations

Authority, 205

Barth, Ernest A. T., on Negro power structure, 76, 102, 176

Bases of power. *See* Power

Bennett, John, on social structure, 25

Black Muslims, as religious sect, 45-46; as potential contenders for leadership, 177n

Bloc voting, Negro, 66, 195

Boss, political, lack of in sub-community, 68

Businessmen, as leaders 53-57. *See also* Economic dominants, Economic institutions, Leader, Negro Business League

Channels of Communication. *See* Communication

Churches, Negro, 39-40, 155. *See also* Communication, Ministers, Religious institutions

Communication, problem of in biracial setting, 16, 151, 166-67; between Negro leaders and sub-

community, 37, 82, 151-55; role of churches in, 45; on specific issues, 111-12, 124-25, 131-36 *passim*, 157-62; channels of, 111-21 *passim*, 129-31, 143, 155, 162-67, 187-88; definition of, 201. *See also* Interaction, Organizations

Community, as research setting, 4, 14; definition of, 201. *See also* Crescent City, Negro sub-community

Conservative leadership. *See* Accommodative leadership

Controversial issues. *See* Issues

Cosmopolitan leader, 50, 55, 149. *See also* Functional leader

Crescent City, location of, 4-5, 18; biracial structure of, 5, 24; ecological development, 18-19; economic and political organization in, 19-21; attitude of citizens toward, 21-22; sub-community in, 22-24, 162; class structure of, 28-29; issues and policy in, 124-47; power structure of, 189, 190-93. *See also* Ecology, Negro sub-community

Crescent City Board of Education, policy on desegregation, 111, 131-32, 133-34, 139-40, 141

Crescent City Commission on Race Relations, grass roots organization of, 126-28; passage through city council, 128; Negro reaction to, 129-31; white reaction to, 131, 164; role in community issues, 132, 145, 147

Crescent City Council, make-up of, 120-21; Negro members of, 70, 71, 118-20; candidates for, 118-22
Crescent City Merchants Association, boycott of, 145
Crescent Negro Council, role of education committee, 47, 48, 133, 134-35; actions in protest demonstrations, 56, 144, 145, 146; role of economic committee, 58; role of political action committee, 67, 72; as coordinating body for sub-committee organizations, 72-73; part played in community issues, 122-47 *passim;* as communication channel, 154, 155

Dahl, Robert, on integrated community, 99
Davis, Kingsley, on status and office, 204
Decisions, definition of, 202
Decision-maker, 147-50; relationship to power nominees, 108, 148-49; as related to decisions, 202. *See also* Leader, Power leader
Decision-making, 110-43; use of desegregation issues to observe, 14-15; communal interests served by sub-community decision-making, 151-52; as result of power status, 202
De Gré, Gerard, on pluralistic societies, 12n
Democratic party, Negro participation in, 50, 65-66, 70
Desegregation, as decision-making issue, 14-15; effects of United States Supreme Court decision on, 15, 46, 196; white community action against, 52, 124-26, 131-32, 139, 171-72; in various community institutions and organizations, 110-18, 146-47, 164, 168, 194; of schools, 124-46 *passim*

Ecology, 18-19; Negro, 22-24, 74, 105-6
Economic dominants, Negro, place in power structure, 11, 184, 191; inheritance of prestige positions, 53-54; as power nominees, 54-55, 103; as race leaders, 181, 182-83, 184-85; as power leaders, 191; definition of, 204. *See also* Leader, Economic institutions
Economic institutions, Negro, 23-24, 30, 52-57; inter-dependency of with other institutions, 26, 41, 48-49, 66-68; dominance of old upper-class families, 30-31, 52-53; small commercial enterprises, 55-56
Economic power, 10-12. *See also* Power
Education, and Negro social mobility, 31, 46, 51; class differences in, 32-36 *passim*
Educational institutions, Negro, 46-52; college, 48-49; academic personnel as leaders, 49-50, 103, 118, 135

Family, Negro, social class differences in, 30-37 *passim;* pioneering families, 30-31, 52, 53; structure of, 38-39
Frazier, E. Franklin, 3, 29; on functional Negro leader, 17, 177, 181; on black bourgeoisie, 33
Functional leader, 182-83. *See also* Frazier, E. Franklin; Moderate race leadership; Race leader

Goals, 51-52, 109, 149-50, 157, 191; shift in methods for achieving, 138-39, 142-43, 166, 174

Haer, John L., 161
Health. *See* Medical profession
Hunter, Floyd, 105, 176; on Negro power structure, 76, 103; on communication and interaction, 76, 151